PERSONAL REVIVAL

God's Way of Setting Our Hearts on Fire

by

S.J. HILL

S. J. Hill
P. O. Box 918
Grandview, MO 64030
www.sjhill.com

ISBN 0-9673378-0-1

Book design and production by Write Hand Publishing
www.writehand.com

CONTENTS

DEDICATION

This book is dedicated to Jonathan and Lance, my two sons whom I love more than they will ever know, and also to their generation. May the love of Christ so capture their hearts that they will passionately love Him and radically serve Him all of their lives. May they experience the power, presence and glory of God like no other generation.

ACKNOWLEDGMENTS

I would like to thank Janet Willig for her labor of love in editing the original manuscript. She will always be a part of whatever impact this book may have on the lives of others.

I want to express my love and appreciation to my parents for their godly example over the years — to my dad (who has since gone on to be with the Lord), for truly demonstrating the Father's heart to the hurting and needy, and to my mother for her incredible ability to always give of herself on behalf of others.

I would like to thank my wife, Pam, for her loving support throughout the years of our marriage and ministry together. Only she fully understands the pain and joy of serving Christ with me. Pam, I will always love you!

Most of all, thank you Heavenly Father, for your incredible love for me; and, Jesus, for willingly paying the ultimate price for someone like me; and, precious Holy Spirit, for never giving up on me!

FOREWORD

If there is one thing I have learned in the last twenty-eight years it is that everything flows out of our personal relationship with the Lord, that the inner life is more essential than the outward life, that our private walk with God is more important than our public ministry for God, that personal revival takes precedence over corporate revival. After all, the Body of Christ is made up of individuals, and it will never be stronger as a unit than it is individually.

Yet it is so tempting to put all our emphasis on the works of ministry—preaching, teaching, pastoring, leading worship, leading a home group, witnessing, visiting the sick, being godly parents, going on missions trips, making disciples—and it is so easy to neglect our private devotion to the Lord. (A more subtle temptation is to spend all our private time in prayer and the Word preparing for our public, outward ministry responsibilities.) What about intimacy with Jesus for the sake of intimacy? What about deepening our relationship with the Master simply for the sake of that relationship? What about pursuing the imitation of God in our lives as a goal in itself and not just as a tool for more effective ministry?

The problem, of course, is that the responsibilities of life and ministry often carry us along with the force of their demands, driving us *to action* and *away from* devotion, pushing us to work for the Lord but pulling us away from waiting on the Lord. How can we resist this tendency? How can we make our relationship with

God the highest priority of our lives? How can we experience personal revival, and how can we sustain that life of passion, fire, and renewal?

In this important, clearly written book by S.J. Hill, you will find both inspiration as well as practical instruction. Drawing on a wide range of edifying sources, and writing from years of personal experience, S J. (also known to many as Steve) has put together a fine biblical study that will help every believer who is hungry for a deeper and closer walk with Jesus. You will be stirred and helped as you read the pages that follow!

Of course, our works for the Lord *are* important. We are called to win souls, to set captives free, to bear fruit that will last, to make an impact for the King. But if our foundations are not secure and our roots are not deep, many of our works will go up in flames. And that's why *Personal Revival* is such a practical and essential book: It points the way to successful ministry *built on the foundation* of a revived and broken heart.

You see, it is possible to backslide while preaching to thousands. It is possible to grow cold while serving in a red-hot revival. It is possible to leave your first love while working for Jesus on the mission field. And that is what makes this book so valuable, since it provides meat for the mature and solid food for the serious, showing us the way to maintain personal revival in the valley as well as on the mountain top. It is my joy to commend *Personal Revival* to you. If you read it and digest it you will be revived and you will stay revived.

Dr. Michael Brown

INTRODUCTION

Gypsy Smith, the English evangelist, was once asked the secret of revival. His reply: "Go home. Take a piece of chalk. Draw a circle around yourself. Then pray, 'O Lord, revive everything inside this circle.'"[1]

While much has been written over the years on the subject of revival, many of us as Christians have lost hope of seeing a real move of God during our lifetime. Thinking that revival can only come in great earth-shaking outpourings of the Spirit, we have overlooked the fact that it is first and foremost a personal experience. When God revives His people, He has to start with someone because the Church only consists of individual believers. Where else can spiritual renewal take place but in the lives of individuals? The Church is not a building! There is no abstract "Church" which can be revived apart from the men and women who make up the Church.

For us to have revival in our generation, we are going to have to do far more than merely think of it in general terms. Each of us must take personal responsibility to cry out for a fresh, radical encounter with the Living Christ. The refining fire of God must consume the impotency of our own lives before we can ever expect it to spread to an indifferent world.

Are we willing to face the searching questions of Charles Finney, the great revivalist of the 19th century? "If God should ask you this moment, by an audible voice from heaven, 'Do you want a revival?' Would you dare to say, Yes? 'Are you willing to make the sacrifices?' Would you answer, Yes? 'When shall it begin?' Would you answer, Let it begin today—let it begin here—let it begin in my heart now?'"[1]

The story is told of a man named David Dodge who found himself in a conversation with a devout Quaker. This man, like Mr. Dodge, was longing to see revival. The two of them agreed that what was needed was more enthusiasm, prayer and consecration. However, after further thought, the Quaker realized that something else would be required and suggested, "Friend Dodge, suppose thee and I make a beginning!"[3]

Little did the Quaker realize the importance of what he had said—"Suppose thee and I make a beginning." This is always a major key to spiritual breakthrough! We must never forget that "I" is always central to the word "revival." When we understand this principle, we cannot help but be encouraged! Nothing can keep us from the revival we so desperately need if we want it badly enough. Each of us who desires God's best will immediately become the focus of the personal care and attention of the Holy Spirit. Regardless of the spiritual environment that surrounds us, the Spirit of God will deal with our hearts as exclusively as if no others existed.

Let each of us, therefore, determine afresh to hold nothing back from Christ, so we can become carriers of revival wherever we may be, allowing the Spirit of God to fan the flame worldwide!

'I saw a human life, ablaze with God;

I felt a power Divine,

As through an empty vessel of frail clay

I saw God's glory shine.

Then woke I from a dream, and cried aloud:

"My Father, give to me

The blessing of a life consumed by fire,

Let me burn out for Thee"'!

Author Unknown

Chapter One

HEARTS ON FIRE

The year was 1738. England was in an extremely dark period of her history. The spiritual state of the country was at an all-time low. The era was once described as follows: "The whole population seemed to be given over to an orgy of drunkenness which made the very name of Englishmen to stink in the nostrils of other nations." It was normal to see signs outside the pubs that read, "Drunk for a penny. Dead drunk for two. Straw to lie on."[1]

The theatre was also disgustingly obscene and corrupt. Literature of the period would have been classified as pornographic. Fornication, homosexuality and polygamy were considered common. Violence went unchecked as gangs of drunken thugs prowled the streets committing horrible crimes!

England would have plummeted to her destruction had it not been for a young man named John Wesley attending a meeting at Aldersgate Street on May 24th of that pivotal year, and feeling his own heart "strangely warmed."

John Wesley had become a missionary to Britain's colony of Georgia in America in 1735. By the year 1738, a very frustrated Wesley had decided to end his ministry in America and sail back to England. He wrote in his journal, "I went to America to convert the Indians; but oh, who shall convert me?"[2]

Upon returning home, he was later invited to a Christian meeting where someone read Luther's preface to the Book of Romans. In recalling his experience, Wesley wrote, "About a quarter to nine, while he was describing the change which God works in the heart through faith in Christ, I felt my heart strangely warmed. I felt I did trust in Christ, Christ alone for salvation; and an assurance was given me that He had taken away my sins, even mine, and saved me from the law of sin and death."[3]

The course of a nation was drastically altered because one man had a heart-warming! John Wesley did more to change England than all the experts and reformers of his day. The legacy of Wesley reads as follows: "John Wesley left six silver spoons and the Methodist Church." What a heritage! Maximum spiritual accomplishment with minimal material possessions!

THE REVIVAL OF 1857

At noon on September 23, 1857, a tall, middle-aged former businessman ascended to the third story of an old church building in the heart of lower New York City. He entered an empty room, pulled out his pocket watch and sat down to wait. The sign outside read: "Prayer Meeting from 12 to 1 o'clock—Stop 5, 10, or 20 minutes, or the whole hour, as your time admits." It appeared as though no one had the time. As the minutes ticked away, the lone man wondered if all his efforts had been in vain.

For three long months he had visited boarding houses, offices and shops, inviting people to the Old Dutch North Church at Fulton and Williams Streets. Attendance was slowly dwindling. Many families in the neighborhood had moved away. Other churches had relocated. Many thought that the Old Dutch North Church should close its doors, but the trustees, looking for a solution to their dilemma, hired a man to conduct a visitation program. Jeremiah C. Lamphier, a 49 year-old merchant with no experience in church visitation, gave up his job in order to knock on doors for less than $1,000 a year. Often Lamphier returned to his room deeply discouraged because of the lack of spiritual interest seen in the people he visited. Yet he never failed to draw new strength from his time of prayer with the Lord.

One day, while visiting some of the neighborhoods, the thought occurred to him that businessmen might want to get away for a short time of prayer once a week at noon. After obtaining permission from church officials, Lamphier passed out handbills and put up the sign. However, he was the only one present as the first meeting began on that early fall day.

He waited ten minutes, then ten minutes more. As his watch read 12:30, he heard footsteps coming up the stairs. One man walked in, then another and another until there were six. The first small prayer meeting was in no way extraordinary. There was no real stirring of the Holy Spirit. Still, the men decided that they would meet again the following Wednesday.

Twenty men came to the second noon-hour prayer meeting. The Holy Spirit honored their diligence and hunger for revival and soon the "Fulton Street" meeting became a daily occurrence, with more than 3,000 people in attendance.

Within six months, 10,000 businessmen (out of a population of 800,000) were gathering daily in New York City for prayer. By January of 1858, some twenty other prayer meetings were flourishing, many of them started by the YMCA.

Newspapers began to assign reporters to cover the prayer meetings. Many outstanding cases of conversion and personal revival were reported in detail. The headlines were flashed from coast to coast.

Early in 1858, the revival blessings from these prayer meetings spilled over the Appalachian Mountains and into the West. Every major city felt its effects. In one of Charles Finney's meetings in Boston, a man stood to his feet and said, "I am from Omaha in Nebraska. On my journey east I found a continuous prayer meeting all the way. We call it 2,000 miles from Omaha to Boston; so I have witnessed a prayer meeting 2,000 miles in extent."[4]

By the summer of 1859, news of the prayer meetings had crossed the Atlantic Ocean. The revival surged on into 1860 until it was scattered, although not stopped, by the Civil War.

Little did Jeremiah Lamphier realize that what was birthed in his own heart would be the beginning of a great national revival which would sweep an estimated one million people into the Kingdom of God.

THE ULSTER REVIVAL

In the same month that Jeremiah Lamphier started the Fulton Street prayer meeting in New York City, four young Irishmen began a weekly prayer meeting in their home country's northernmost province of Ulster. This meeting is commonly regarded as the origin of the 1859 revival that swept 100,000 converts into the churches of Ireland.

One of the young men was James McQuilkin, who was converted in 1856 through the witness of a godly woman. McQuilkin later read George Mueller's autobiography, *THE LIFE OF TRUST*, and was deeply impressed by Mueller's life of prayer and faith. McQuilkin asked the Lord for a spiritual companion with whom he could pray, and God gave him one. After the two began to meet together, two more young men were added to their small prayer group. McQuilkin told his friends about the inspiration he had received through reading about Mueller and encouraged them to continue in prayer. For several months, very little seemed to happen. Yet, the four young men faithfully persevered.

When James McQuilkin heard about the revival in America, he said to himself, "Why may we not have such a blessed work here?" He shared his burden with his three friends and the fire in their hearts consumed them. In answer to their prayers, the first conversion of an individual to Christ took place in December of 1857. From that time on it was reported that "Humble, grateful, loving, joyous converts multiplied."[5] The prayer meetings became crowded. Revival fires started to spread! J. Edwin Orr, the great Church historian, said that this revival "which originated in a prayer meeting of four young men in the village schoolhouse of Kells made greater impact spiritually on Ireland than anything else known since the days of Saint Patrick."[6]

THE WELSH REVIVAL

Evan Roberts was born in Loughor, Wales, in 1878. After working for some time as both a miner and blacksmith, he entered grammar school at Newcastle-Emlyn to prepare for the ministry. Even in those days, God gave him an insatiable hunger for revival.

For thirteen years Evan had prayed for the Spirit and often thought of the words of William Davies, the deacon, who said, "Remember to be faithful. What if the Spirit descended and you were absent? Remember Thomas! What a loss he had."

In response to Davie's admonition, Evan wrote: "I said to myself: 'I will have the Spirit'; and through every kind of weather and in spite of all difficulties, I went to the meetings. Many times, on seeing other boys with the boats on the tide, I was tempted to turn back and join them. But, no, I said to myself: 'Remember your resolve,' and on I went. I went faithfully to the meetings for prayer throughout the ten or eleven years I prayed for a Revival. It was the Spirit that moved me thus to think."

In September of 1904, while still attending school, Evan went to a conference at a place called Blaenanerch. These meetings were initiated to consider the spiritual life of the churches in the area and to decide what action should be taken. It was during this conference that Evan was filled with the Holy Spirit.

At a certain morning meeting which Evan attended, the evangelist that was speaking asked the Lord to "bend" them. The Holy Spirit seemed to say to Roberts, "That's what you need, to be bent." In describing his experience, he said, "I felt a living force coming into my bosom. This grew and grew, and I was almost bursting. My bosom was boiling. I fell on my knees with my arms over the seat in front of me; the tears and perspiration flowed freely. I thought blood was gushing forth." Several friends approached him to wipe his face, but he continued crying out, "O Lord, bend me! Bend me!"

Roberts went on to say, "After I was bent, a wave of peace came over me, and the audience sang, 'I hear Thy welcome voice.' And as they sang I thought about the bending at the Judgment Day, and I was filled with compassion for those that would have to bend on that day, and I wept. Henceforth, the salvation of souls became the burden of my heart. From that time I was on fire with a desire to go through all Wales, and if it were possible, I was willing to pray God for the privilege of going."[7]

From then on, this twenty-six year old went everywhere spreading the fires of revival. The chapels were crowded, with hundreds more outside. His appearance at these meetings caused a lot of excitement, and Roberts needed only to say a few words of exhortation or a brief prayer to set the congregations on fire. The people would break out into singing and then testimony, followed by prayer, and then singing again. It was said that "...all of Wales seemed like a praise meeting." Mealtimes and other daily routines were neglected as God moved throughout the entire country in saving and purifying power. Revival had come to Wales! And it all started with a young man who was prepared to pray, "**O Lord, bend me! Bend me!**"

THE HEBRIDES REVIVAL

Early in a winter morning in 1949, in a little cottage near Barvas Village on the Isle of Lewis in the Scottish Hebrides (off Scotland's western coast), an eighty-four year old blind woman named Peggy Smith, and her sister, Christine, gathered in fervent prayer.

On this particular morning God visited the two of them in a special way, giving them an unusual assurance that the revival for which they had been passionately praying was close at hand. Several months before, Peggy had had a dream in which she was shown that revival was coming and the churches would be crowded again with young people.

At the time, revival seemed almost impossible. World War II had taken its toll. Many had left the islands to serve in the armed forces, and some had never returned. Those who did come back after the war returned confused and disillusioned. By 1949, the younger generation had very little interest in spiritual matters.

After her dream, Peggy sent for her pastor, James Murray MacKay, and told him of her experience. She asked him to call the leaders of the church to prayer. For three months, he and others met three nights a week to seek God for revival. On one occasion, these men gathered together at 10 p.m. in a barn in the town of Barvas. Kneeling in the straw, they cried out to the Lord for an outpouring of His Spirit. During their time of prayer, a young deacon from the Free Church stood up and read Psalm 24:3,4: "Who may ascend the hill of the Lord? Who may stand in his holy place? He who has clean hands and a pure heart, who does not lift up his soul to an idol or swear by what is false." He read the verses again and then said to the group, "Brethren, we have been praying for weeks, waiting on God. But I would like to ask now: Are our hands clean? Is the heart pure?"

As the men continued to seek the Lord, His awesome presence swept into the barn. At four in the morning, it was said, "They moved out of the realm of the common and the natural into the sphere of the supernatural."

Pastor MacKay then felt led to invite Duncan Campbell, the well-known Scottish evangelist, to Barvas for special meetings. His invitation was confirmed by Peggy Smith, who told him that "one night in a vision the Lord had revealed to her not only that revival was coming, but also the identity of the instrument He had chosen to use—Duncan Campbell."

Yet, Duncan Campbell told them that it was impossible for him to come because he was preparing for a convention. When the two praying sisters heard of his reply, they simply said, "That is what man has said. God has said he is coming, and he will be here within the fortnight" [two weeks]—and he was.

A real sense of expectation pervaded Duncan Campbell's first service in the Barvis Presbyterian church. However, nothing unusual took place, although it was a good meeting. Afterwards, a deacon of the church said to Duncan, "Do not be discouraged; He is coming. I hear already the rumblings of heaven's chariot wheels." Then the man suggested to the already tired preacher that they go and spend the night in prayer! Approximately thirty people went with them to a nearby cottage.

Later, Duncan Campbell described what happened: "God was beginning to move, the heavens were opening, we were there on our faces before God. Three o'clock in the morning came, and GOD SWEPT IN. About a dozen men and women lay prostrate on the floor, speechless. Something had happened; we knew that the forces of darkness were going to be driven back, and men were going to be delivered. We left the cottage at 3 A.M. to discover men and women seeking God. I walked along a country road, and found three men on their faces, crying to God for mercy. There was a light in every home; no one seemed to think of sleep."[8] Revival had begun!

Although the revival peaked between 1949 and 1952, the results were still evident for a number of years. Many young men who were deeply impacted by the outpouring of the Holy Spirit entered the ministry, while others answered the call to the world's mission fields. All this took place because two elderly women, one blind and the other severely crippled with arthritis, desired to see revival come in their lifetime and would not let go of God in prayer!

Duncan Campbell wrote, "Those who seek God for revival must be prepared for God to work in His own way and not according to their programme. But His sovereignty does not relieve men of responsibility; God is the God of revival but man is the human agent through whom revival is possible. Desire for revival is one thing; confident anticipation that our desire will be fulfilled is another."[9]

This truth was never more clearly demonstrated than in the life of a man by the name of Jonathan Goforth. After serving as a missionary in China for some time in the late 1800's, he came to the conclusion that God had more for him than what he was experiencing in both his personal life and ministry. He became restless and was led by the Holy Spirit into an intense study of the Scriptures concerning the subject of revival. "Every passage that had any bearing upon the price of, or the road to the accession of power became life and breath to me," he said.[10] After months of soul-searching study, he came to believe that God would fulfill His Word, even in the face of the incredible odds that were against him in the land of China.

When the Spirit of God eventually fell upon the people of Manchuria in an awesome way, a Chinese evangelist later asked Goforth why he had not told them that there was going to be revival. In deep humility, the missionary confessed that he had not known revival was even possible until it had actually touched his own life.

SPREADING THE FIRE

When personal revival comes to individual men and women and sets their hearts on fire, it automatically spreads. Fire spreads upward and outward, building and growing until it consumes everything in its path. Such was the case in the life of Jonathan Edwards, one of the greatest theologians America has ever produced.

In 1724, during one of the mightiest awakenings to hit the North American Continent, Jonathan Edwards, after much prayer and fasting, begged Christians of all lands to unite together in prayer for a world-wide revival and to return to radical New Testament Christianity.

A copy of his famous appeal fell into the hands of William Carey, an English shoemaker. Carey, deeply moved by what he read, assembled a small group of believers in his home to pray that God would do a "new thing" in their midst. Carey republished Edwards' revival appeal, and as a result, a world-wide missionary movement was birthed. William Carey later came to be known as the father of modern missions.

God also used Edwards' call for revival to change the spiritual life of Charles Finney, a converted lawyer from New York State. Finney would come to base many of his ideas about revival on this one document. Jonathan Edwards' burden for revival lit a fire in the heart of this young man, and as a result of his evangelistic meetings the flames spread throughout North America!

Years later, while on vacation in the Mediterranean, Finney became so burdened about the spiritual condition of the churches in America that he began to prepare his now famous *LECTURES ON REVIVAL*. These lectures have been read by Christians all over the world, and through their message revival has come to many individual lives and churches.

When we read of famous people such as John Wesley, Evan Roberts and Charles Finney, we might assume that all revivals began with well-known personalities. However, most revivals began with obscure, unknown individuals. How many of us had ever heard of Peggy Smith, Jeremiah Lamphier, James MacKay or James McQuilkin?

Even those whose names later became synonymous with certain revivals never considered themselves "special." In fact, none made any significant impact on those around them until they had gone through a season of personal revival! It was out of their own desperation that their hearts were set on fire and the lives of others deeply impacted!

God has called each of us to fulfill a specific mission in life. It does not matter whether we are young or old, educated or uneducated. We may be a housewife, businessman or blue-collar worker. Yet, every one of us has been born into the Kingdom for such a time as this (Esther 4:14). Our lives can make a difference! Destiny beats in the heart of every one of us! None of us is insignificant!

What is "insignificant" to the Lord, anyway? A weather-beaten stick became "the rod of God" in the hands of Moses. Samson used the jawbone of a donkey to kill a thousand Philistines. Gideon's little band of 300 men destroyed 135,000 Midianites with all of their armed might. 1 Corinthians 1:28 informs us that "God chose things despised by the world, things counted as nothing at all, and used them to bring to nothing what the world considers important" (New Living Translation). These are the amazing ways of the Lord!

ALIVE TO FULFILL THE CREATOR'S PURPOSE

One beautiful morning a very strange conversation took place in the woods. While there were many who looked on and listened, there were just four voices heard to speak. A tiny white lily waved in the breeze by the trickling brook. High above her towered the branches of a gnarled old oak tree.

"Are you not ashamed of yourself, little flower," exclaimed the mighty oak. "When you see how big I am, do you not feel insignificant; while my branches spread far out in every direction, you fill such a small place in this world."

"No," replied the lily. "We are both just what God made us. And to each of us He has given a gift: fragrance to me and strength to you."

"Where will your sweetness be a few days from now?" asked the oak scornfully. "You will soon wither and decay, and your grave will not lift the ground higher by a blade of grass. But I shall live on for years—perhaps even for centuries. And when I am cut down, I may be built into a mighty ship to carry men over the sea; or perhaps I shall be fashioned into a coffin that will hold the body of a prince or a king. Ah, little frail lily, what is your lot in comparison to mine?"

Now while the oak was taunting the lily, a little brown squirrel sitting on the lowest branch of the oak had been most attentive to their conversation. Indeed he was quite impressed by the boasting of the mighty oak, but he was equally alert to the gentle confidence of the little lily as it spoke to the oak.

"It is true," replied the lily humbly, "that I am small and frail, and that I shall not live long. But if I live fragrantly I will have added my small bit of beauty and enjoyment to the world. I shall then have filled the complete purpose of the One who sent me—my Creator; and that is all that really matters to me."

Just then another listening ear could hold her voice no longer. It was the tiny raindrop whose voice burst forth announcing: "Please do not think me rude if I intrude, for truly I am the smallest of all; so very, very small beside the oak, yes, even small beside the lily or the squirrel. But I am sure that I have learned the wondrous secret of living."

The tiny raindrop knew that every ear was tuned, for all were interested in knowing this secret. "When I am sent by my Creator on my long journey down to earth, I approach with just one thing in view: to fulfill His purpose in sending me. Oh mighty oak, my life seems so very short as I wash your leaves and bark, and soak your thirsty roots. Oh little squirrel, I love to wash your glossy coat of fur and, purchance, even to quench your inner thirst. Oh, lovely lily, I always hope that I can fall upon you to freshen and release your gracious fragrance. I love

25

to be near you, for you also seem so content with fulfilling our Creator's purpose. That must be the reason why you are always looking up to HIM."

At last the little squirrel was fully convinced, and it was time for him to speak: "Oh mighty oak, beside you, I, too, have always felt so very insignificant until this morning. Suddenly I remembered that many, many generations ago one of my family planted a small acorn from which you grew. Is it not wonderful that our Creator placed this instinct within in my breast that I too might fulfill His purpose in my being?"

That morning as the meeting broke up, you could hear the mighty oak tree leading every member of the forest in this triumphant chorus: "HOW WONDERFUL TO BE ALIVE, ESPECIALLY WHEN YOU ARE ALIVE TO FULFILLING THE CREATOR'S PURPOSE!"[11]

SEND THE FIRE

Thou Christ of burning, cleansing flame,
Send the fire!
Thy Blood-bought gift today we claim,
Send the fire!
Look down and see this waiting host,
Give us the promised Holy Ghost,
We want another Pentecost,
Send the fire!

God of Elijah hear our cry!
Send the fire!
Oh, make us fit to live or die,
Send the fire!
To burn up every trace of sin,
To bring the light and glory in,
The revolution now begin,
Send the fire!

'Tis fire we want, for fire we plead,
Send the fire!
The fire will meet our ev'ry need,
Send the fire!
For daily strength to do the right,
For grace to conquer in the fight,
For power to walk the world in white,
Send the fire!

To make our weak hearts strong and brave,
Send the fire!
To live a dying world to save;
Send the fire!
Oh, see us on Thy altar lay
Our lives, our all, this very day;
To crown the off'ring now, we pray,
Send the fire!

General William Booth

Chapter Two
REVIVAL DEFINED

Personal revival—this may seem like a rather odd phrase, especially in light of the way most of us view the subject. Because the word "revival" has been used in a number of ways over the years, the term itself carries with it a variety of meanings.

For many of us, revival has become synonymous with special meetings. It is common for churches in many parts of the world to "hold" revivals. We often see signs stating: REVIVAL—ONE WEEK ONLY or REVIVAL EVERY NIGHT THIS WEEK. While these signs are an indication of special meetings which have been scheduled weeks and even months in advance, any meeting which men plan and conduct at their own choosing cannot honestly be called a "revival."

Revival is also often equated with mass evangelism. As important as evangelism is, this aspect of ministry does not define revival's true nature. While the salvation of the lost should be a by-product of revival, evangelism is what men do for the cause of Christ. Revival, on the other hand, is what Christ does for the sake of His people.

Church growth is also considered to be tantamount to revival. Many churches are following carefully detailed plans and programs, hoping to see some consistent increase in attendance. Any measure of success is often viewed as proof of spiritual life and vitality. However, this is not necessarily the case. If we simply equate church growth with revival, we will miss the ultimate reality of what God is wanting to perform within human hearts.

Revivals have even come to be known as religious, emotional extravaganzas with big tents, large crowds and loud music! These meetings, sad to say, have often been associated with sensationalism, commercialism and showmanship. Such extremes, however, have little or nothing to do with genuine revival!

If every series of special meetings can be called a "revival," then how are we going to be able to pray intelligently for the real thing? If revival is the pressing need of the hour, we must rediscover the true meaning of the word!

What, then, is the essence of true revival, and where does it initially begin? The real nature of revival can never be adequately described by just one definition. As one minister so aptly said, "Revival in a definition is like David in Saul's armour—it just doesn't fit." Revival can no more be confined to a mere definition or formula than anything else that is God-sent. However, we can discover from Scripture, as well as from history, the legitimate nature of revival.

Although the Bible does not specifically mention the word "revival," it does use the term "revive," which comes from the Hebrew word "chayah" (khawyaw), and can also be translated "to live, make alive, recover, repair, restore." The general sense of the verb "to revive" usually means "to quicken" or "to impart fresh life." By looking at various references throughout the Old Testament, we can find different forms of the word "chayah" and come away with a comprehensive picture of what God is eager to do in each of our lives.

For example, in Hosea 14:7, the promise made to those who return to the Lord is "...They shall be **revived** like grain."* This phrase colorfully portrays the idea of something that is flourishing and illustrates for us what happens when lives are revived by the Spirit of God!

In 1 Chronicles 11:8, we read that "...Joab **repaired** the rest of the city."* The word "repaired" is from the same root word we have been studying and offers us another vivid example of the essence of revival.

Further applications of the word "chayah" suggest the idea of **recovery** and **restoration.** The recovery may be from depression or discouragement, as in the case of Jacob. We read in Genesis 45:25-27 that his sons "... went up out of Egypt, and came to the land of Canaan to Jacob their father. And they told him, saying, 'Joseph is still alive, and he is governor over all the land of Egypt.' And Jacob's heart stood still, because he did not believe them. But when they told him all the words which Joseph had said to them, and when he saw the carts which Joseph had sent to carry him, the spirit of Jacob their father **revived.**"*

The recovery may also be from sheer thirst and exhaustion, as mentioned in Judges 15:18-19, when Samson, after slaying a thousand men with the jaw-bone of an ass, became extremely thirsty. "So God split the hollow place that is in Lehi, and water came out, and he drank; and his spirit returned, and **he revived.**"* The restoration may also be from slavery, as suggested in Ezra 9:8, when the priest offered thanks to the Lord for giving them a measure of revival in their bondage.

Often the recovery spoken of is from sickness and disease. When the children of Israel were bitten by fiery serpents in the desert, Moses was instructed to make a serpent of brass and lift it up before the people. "And it came to pass, that if a serpent had bitten any man, when he beheld the serpent of brass, he **lived**"* (Numbers 21:9). A spin-off from this same verb is used in the story of Naaman's healing from leprosy (2 Kings 5:7), as well as in Elisha's prophecy concerning Benhadad's recovery from sickness (2 Kings 8:10).

Other forms of the Hebrew word "chayah" appear in passages which describe **resuscitation** from physical death. In 2 Kings 8:5

and 13:21, the Scriptures depict the "reviving" of both the Shunammite's son and the man who was buried in the tomb of Elisha. In the case of the widow's son who died at Zarephath, we read that when "...the soul of the child came back to him, ...he **revived**"* (1 Kings 17:22). Even the resurrection of dry bones mentioned in Ezekiel 37 further portrays the true nature of revival. We read in verse 10 that when the "breath [spirit] came into them, ...they **lived,** and stood upon their feet, an exceedingly great army."*

The Psalms also abound with references to revival, individual as well as corporate. Psalm 80:18-19, for example, is still relevant for the reviving of God's people today. "Then we will not turn back from you; **Revive** us, and we will call upon your name. **Restore** us, O Lord God of hosts; Cause Your face to shine, and we shall be saved."* In Psalm 85:6 the question is raised, "Will You not **revive** us again, that Your people may rejoice in You?"* The 119th Psalm is also filled with examples relating to personal revival. Nine times the Psalmist prays, "**Revive me**"* (Psalm 19:25,37,40,88,107,149, 154,156,159).

This plea for personal revival echoes throughout the 119th Psalm and brings both an invitation and a challenge to every one of us. It directs us to the only way of blessing! Before we can ever expect corporate revival within the Church, each of us must be willing to pray, "**Revive me,** O Lord."

In looking at the expanding word picture the Scriptures have painted for us, we see that God is longing to revive His people so they can grow up and flourish as a holy habitation in which He can dwell. He is seeking to repair the walls around the Church, as well as our own individual lives, so there will again be a line of demarcation between the holy and profane, the clean and the unclean.

The Father also desires to revive us in order to deliver us from all discouragement and heaviness so we may freely rejoice in Him. He wants to satisfy our thirst by offering Himself as the Water of

Life. He seeks to free us from every form of bondage and heal us from the terrible disease of sin. He longs to restore life to a dying Church, corporately as well as to areas of our individual spiritual lives that may be weak. Oh, that we would welcome Him, without reservation, to come and do in us what His heart is eager to perform!

As we move into the New Testament, we discover that the Greek equivalent of the Old Testament word for "revive" is found only a few times. The Greek word "anazao" is used for the **restoration** of the prodical son (Luke 15:24,32), the **reviving** of sin (Romans 7:9), the **resurrection** of Christ (Romans 14:9), and the **resurrection** of the dead in the last days (Revelation 20:5).

A related Greek word "anazapureo" means "to stir up" or "rekindle a fire which is slowly dying." It also means "to keep in full flame." This word is used metaphorically in 2 Timothy 1:6, when Paul said to Timothy, "For this reason I remind you to **fan into flame** the gift of God, which is in you through the laying on of my hands"* (New International Version). Another similar Greek word "anathallo" is translated "flourish" in Philippians 4:10, where Paul wrote, "...your care of me has **flourished** again."* Moffat translates this verse, "It was a joy to me in the Lord that your care for me could **revive** again."* The literal meaning of the word is "to put forth fresh shoots." The picture here is of the coming of spring, bringing new life to trees and vegetation, as illustrated in Song of Solomon 2:11-13.

The reason these Greek words are not found more often in the New Testament should be obvious—the Early Church did not need reviving. God's people were immersed in the life and power of the Holy Spirit. However, one of the clearest and simplest portrayals of revival can actually be found in the Book of Acts. Acts 3:19 speaks of "...times of refreshing...from the presence of the Lord." No better description could be given for revival than what is contained in this one verse!

In Romans 13:11, we are given an even more comprehensive picture of what the Scriptures teach about the nature of revival. The Apostle Paul appealed to the believer with the following admonition: "The hour has come for you to wake up from your slumber, because our salvation is nearer than when we first believed" (New International Version). This is the **call** to revival!

In the first epistle of John, we are reminded of the Second Coming of Christ and challenged with these words: "And every one who has this hope in him purifies himself, just as He is pure" (1 John 3:3). This is the **heart** of revival!

Without question, the most ardent cry for revival comes from the lips of Jesus Himself in the Book of Revelation. The last message to the Church is not the Great Commission. The last word of Christ to the Church is "Repent." This is the **means** to revival!

LIVES THAT DEFINED REVIVAL

To further understand the nature of revival, we also need to refer to history and the people who not only wrote about revival but also experienced it themselves. Charles Finney described revival as "...the renewal of the first love of Christians, resulting in the conversion of sinners to God. Revival is nothing less than a new beginning of obedience to God, a breaking of heart and getting down in the dust before Him with deep humility and forsaking of sin. A revival breaks the power of the world and of sin over Christians. The charm of the world is broken and the power of sin is overcome. Truths to which our hearts are unresponsive suddenly become living. Whereas mind and conscience may assent to truth, when revival comes, obedience to the truth is the one thing that matters."[1]

John Bonar, a minister of the Gospel, described revival as "the exchange of the form of godliness for its living power."[2]

In the early 1900's, Joseph Kemp, in a presidential address to the Baptist Union of New Zealand, stated that, "Revival, strictly speaking, means the reanimating of that which is already living but in a state of declension. It has to do principally with the Church as a whole and Christians as individuals."[3]

On the basis of Psalm 85:6, Dr. John Simon, the Methodist historian, described revival as "New life bringing a new joy." He went on to say, "The experiences of the day of Pentecost repeat themselves, and the weary Church finding its lost youth, walks in the morning light of Apostolic days."[4]

G. Campbell Morgan, a powerful English preacher, referred to revival as "...the re-animation of the life of the believer (not the unregenerate as they are dead in sin)...there can only be revival where there is life to revive."[5]

Vance Havner, a well-known American evangelist, character- ized revival as "a work of God's Spirit among His own people...what we call revival is simply New Testament Christianity, the saints getting back to normal."[6]

Probably the most graphic portrayal of revival came from Christmas Evans, the famous Welsh minister. He said, "Revival is God bending down to the dying embers of a fire that is just about to go out, and breathing into it, until it bursts again into flame."[7]

In looking at these various descriptions, we see that revival is the work of God through which He comes to His people, renewing them with His life, and restoring them to radical love and obedience. Revival is the **process** through which the Church is returned to its former power and splendor.

Such a work, however, must **first** begin in the lives of individual believers. A. W. Tozer, a pastor and well-known author, said it best when he wrote,

> Revival may be experienced on three levels...in the individual, the church or the community.
>
> It is impossible to have a community revival where there has not been a church revival, and unless at least a few individuals seek and obtain a spiritual transformation in their own hearts, there can be no hope for their church, for a church is composed of individual Christians.
>
> ...One consequence of our failure to see clearly the true nature of revival is that we wait for years for some supernatural manifestation that never comes, overlooking completely our own individual place in the desired awakening. Whatever God may do for a church must be done in the single unit, the one certain man or woman. Some things can happen only to the isolated, single person; they cannot be experienced en masse.
>
> Three thousand persons were converted at Pentecost, but each one met his sin and his Savior alone. The spiritual birth, like the natural one, is for each one a unique, separate experience shared in by no one. And so with that uprush of resurgent life we call revival. It can come to the individual only. Though a visitation of divine life reaches 75 persons at once [as

among the Moravian Brethren at Dusseldorf], yet it comes to each one singly.

If this should seem to be an unduly individualistic approach to revival, let it be remembered that religion is personal before it can be social. Every prophet, every reformer, every revivalist had to meet God alone before he could help the multitudes. The great leaders who went on to turn thousands to Christ had to begin with God and their own soul. The plain Christian of today must experience personal revival before he can hope to bring renewed spiritual life to his church.[8]

In 1904, Dr. F. B. Meyer and Dr. G. Campbell Morgan travelled together to Cardiff, Wales, to experience firsthand the outpouring of the Spirit during the early days of the Welsh Revival. A policeman was on traffic duty outside the railway station when the two men of God approached him to ask where they could find the revival. The man put his hand on his heart and with a glowing face answered, "Gentleman, it is here."[9]

This is where revival is initially to be found. It is not something that is abstract; just as ripples of water are set in motion by a pebble thrown into a lake, revival starts with the individual and spreads to the ends of the earth!

In my heart, dear Lord, I pray
Send a great revival.
Take me, use me day by day,
Send a great revival.
Power for service, Lord, I crave,
Send a great revival;
Help me some lost soul to save,
Send a great revival.

Give me grace Thy will to do,
Send a great revival,
As I now my vow renew,
Send a great revival.

Thine alone, Lord, I would be,
Send a great revival;
Let it now begin in me,
Send a great revival.

Send a great revival, Lord,
Send a great revival, Lord,
Send a great revival, Lord,
And let it NOW begin in me.

Author Unknown

* Emphasis added

Chapter Three

LIFE AFTER DEATH

In a famous speech before Parliament, Benjamin Disraeli compared his political opponents to some extinct volcanoes he had seen on a tour of the English Empire. From the deck of the ship, he had viewed these once powerful peaks which now emitted only thin wisps of smoke. The mighty fires that had once burned brightly in the hearts of the great mountains were now silent!

A similar comparison can be made between these once-active volcanoes and many of our own lives. While at one time we knew the life and vitality of the Spirit, we now find ourselves in desperate need of fresh fire! Some of us were even a part of churches and movements that initially experienced an incredible amount of spiritual energy and activity. Hearts and lives were constantly being transformed. Yet for reasons we do not fully understand, things gradually changed and the fire of God's presence became just a thin wisp of smoke. As a result, many of us are extremely disillusioned because a lot of our hopes and expectations have gone unfulfilled.

Even our spiritual focus has become unclear! What has made matters more difficult is that most of us have not responded well to all that has taken place around us. We find ourselves painfully angry and confused. We do not know where we are spiritually, why we are there or where we are going. What we do understand, however, is that something has gone dramatically wrong with our safe, familiar surroundings! Our strongest sources of identity and support have now become, in some respects, just painful memories. We also find ourselves disoriented, frightened and even "homesick." Something within us wants to return to the past and simply cling to the things we have known. Inwardly, we desperately long for some sense of security to protect us from all of the changes occurring around us.

When Hezekiah began his reign in Judah and saw the need for a spiritual awakening within the nation, he found himself facing a strange enemy in his effort to restore God's blessing to the people. The "enemy" was an object of worship that was later named Nehushtan. This was no heathen idol fashioned by the enemies of the Lord. Instead, it was the brass serpent that had been made by Moses. The symbol of an amazing miracle of God performed centuries before had become an object of idolatrous worship. The people were actually burning incense to it! In order for Judah to move into the future purpose that God had for her, Hezekiah had to literally **shatter** this symbol of their past (2 Kings 18:4).

In our attempts to remain loyal to the things of the past, some of us have ended up living off its memories. We have become trapped in a time warp! If we are not careful, we will find ourselves ensnared in a subtle form of idolatry, giving our allegiance to past "ministries" and the "symbols" of what they did. This trap is very difficult to detect because there seems to be nothing wrong with honoring men and women of God or the things that were done through them. Yet the best way to honor their memory is to follow their example by having the courage to do something that will impact the Kingdom of God!

Our past is not our future! Instead, it is to be the catapult that launches us into the destiny God has for each one of us. We must carry the mantle and not the bones of those who have gone before us (Genesis 50:25). The Holy Spirit, like Hezekiah, has come to shatter those things in our lives that would prevent us from fulfilling His purpose for us. We dare not sit around the remains of dying embers when God has called us to fervently seek fresh fire!

During seasons of disillusionment, it is also quite easy to plunge into feverish activities to try to bury our pain and confusion. We replace "seeking the Lord" with seminars. We look for the latest ideas and methods to help us cope with our personal problems. We come to believe that what we need are new facts rather than new fire! We even pursue political and social agendas, hoping to make a difference in our communities. However, our greatest need is a fresh infilling of the Holy Spirit! We must put aside our frenzied activities long enough to return to the "Upper Room" (Acts 1:13-2:4).

We dare not look for quick-fixes to solve the spiritual void in our lives. Our emptiness can only be filled as we pray for another personal baptism of fire. We must return to the Lord to ask for a fresh infusion of His Spirit. The God whom we seek is the same God who answers by fire. His power cannot help but overtake the life that has been reduced to only wanting more of Him!

For some of us, however, these words may seem to carry very little impact. The trauma and disappointment we encountered in various groups and churches have left us "spiritually numb." We committed ourselves and gave so much, yet we never fully experienced the reality our hearts craved. Now we do not seem to have the spiritual energy to embrace anything new. Our lives appear to be clouded over with a sense of hopelessness, and our vision, for all intents and purposes, has died!

The disciples must have gone through a similar experience when they found their world crumbling around them. Having been told that someone within their ranks was about to betray the Lord and that the time had come for Jesus to die, they found themselves devastated and overwhelmed! Not knowing what to do or where to go, they followed Christ to Gethsemane. It was in the Garden, while Jesus was praying, that the disciples fell asleep. According to

Luke's account of the incident, their falling asleep was not due to physical exhaustion. Jesus, instead, "...found them sleeping from **sorrow**"* (Luke 22:45). Disheartened and disillusioned, the disciples were spiritually and emotionally drained.

Things were supposed to have turned out differently! Jesus was their Messiah-King! They had experienced firsthand all of the sights and sounds of His triumphal entry into Jerusalem. Surely God had sent Him to overthrow the Roman government and put down the enemies of Israel. Hadn't they been chosen to rule and reign with Christ and help establish His Kingdom on the earth?

What they failed to understand was that the purposes of God are never fulfilled the way we imagine. Whether a particular call on our lives, a prophetic word given to us as individuals, or just the sense of destiny each of us feels as a Christian, we need to realize that many of our expectations have been incomplete, or worse, inaccurate!

Imagination is a precious gift from God; it is one of the attributes that separates us from the rest of His creation. However, it can get us into real trouble if we let it. Ideas born out of our own imagination can lead to false expectations, and unfulfilled expectations will always lead to disillusionment.

John the Baptist, for example, was given a powerful revelation of Jesus Christ as the Lamb of God who would take away the sin of the world (John 1:29). While in prison later, John sent two of his disciples to Jesus to ask Him, "Are You the Coming One, or do we look for another?" Jesus answered and said to them, "Go and tell John the things which you hear and see: The blind receive their sight and the lame walk; the lepers are cleansed and the deaf hear; the dead are raised up and the poor have the gospel preached to them. And blessed is he who is not offended because of Me" (Matthew 11:1-6).

Why was Jesus concerned that John might become offended? To better understand John's dilemma, we need to realize that from an Old Testament perspective, the coming of God's Kingdom was viewed as a single, extraordinary event, an awesome manifestation of God's power which would do away with the wicked kingdoms of this world and fill all the earth with righteousness!

John had announced the coming of the Kingdom of God (Matthew 3:2) as he understood it from the Old Testament. He believed that the Messiah would come and bring a two-fold baptism: some would be baptized in the Holy Spirit and experience the salvation of the Kingdom of God, while others would be baptized with the fire of final judgment (Matthew 3:11)!

But Jesus was not acting like the Messiah whom John had announced. To the Jews, Messiah was expected to be either a conquering Davidic King before whom the enemies of God could not stand or He would be a heavenly, supernatural Being who would come to earth with great power and glory to destroy the wicked and bring the Kingdom of God.

Yet, where was the baptism of the Spirit? Where was the judgment of wickedness? Herod was still ruling in Galilee. Roman legions were continuing to march through Jerusalem. Authority rested in the hands of wicked Pilate, and idolatrous, immoral Rome ruled the world with an iron fist!

John's struggle was the struggle of every devout Jew, including Jesus' closest disciples. In an effort to interpret the life and ministry of Jesus, they could not understand how He could be the Messenger of the Kingdom while sin remained unpunished! They failed to realize that the Kingdom of God was already among them. Instead of coming to destroy human rule, it had come to destroy the rule of Satan. Instead of making changes in the political arena, it was making changes in the spiritual lives of men and women!

What complicated matters even more was the fact that John's ministry probably only lasted about six months, causing him to wrestle with unfulfilled expectations as his life was coming to a close. It was not that John was afraid to die; he simply never dreamed that things would end the way they did! What John was having to face was his own personal disillusionment. It was this issue in John's life that Jesus was more than likely addressing. Jesus was concerned that John would become offended because things had not turned out the way John had expected.

COPING WITH CHANGE

Might some of us be facing a similar situation? How many of us are carrying offenses within our hearts and are even bitter toward the Lord because of unmet expectations? How many of us have even lost all sense of spiritual direction because we are still devastated and disillusioned? Yet for us to break free from the pain of the past and experience a new beginning, it is imperative we understand that the word "disillusionment" comes from the word "illusion." Illusion is a belief, concept or opinion that is not in harmony with the facts. Some of the very things we embraced and defended as being a part of God's plan for our lives were birthed out of our own imaginations! Over the years, we innocently developed ideas and concepts that became interwoven with the true purposes of God. We came to believe certain things would happen that were never born out of the heart of our heavenly Father. In fact, some of our ideas and opinions have actually become the "roadblocks" preventing us from fulfilling our God-given destinies.

What we need to realize is that in the midst of our confusion and pain God is actually directing our lives, releasing us from our own agendas and false expectations. He is in the process of removing from us everything that would seek to control Him. He is cutting away attitudes and ideas which have limited His ability to change us. He is forcing our disillusionment to the surface in order to free us from our illusions!

Even though it appears that God is allowing our dreams to die, He is actually in the process of giving life to the things He purposed for us from the beginning! This was never more clearly illustrated than in the lives of Abraham and his long promised son. Abraham was an old man when Isaac was born. From the first moment Isaac was cradled in his father's arms, he immediately became the joy and delight of Abraham's life. This is not difficult to understand, considering that the child represented everything sacred to his father's heart:

> Isaac was born of God and of promise,
>
> He was the anointed son,
>
> He was the hope of the future, and
>
> He was to be the instrument of blessing to others.

As Isaac grew older, the heart of Abraham was knit closer and closer to the life of his son. It was at this point that God stepped in and said to Abraham, "Take now your son, your only son Isaac, whom you love, and go to the land of Moriah, and offer him there as a burnt offering on one of the mountains of which I shall tell you" (Genesis 22:2).

It was there on one of the mountains near Beersheba that Abraham wrestled in agony with God! What a sacred and solemn occasion—so sacred, the Scriptures are silent about what actually took place on that dark, painful night! We can only imagine how Abraham felt as he faced the stark reality that he was not only going to lose Isaac but that all of his hopes, aspirations and dreams were going to die with his son as well. How could he reconcile the act of putting his son to death with the promise God had made to him that he would father a powerful nation through Isaac?

God was testing Abraham to see whom he loved most, his son or his Savior. Yet out of his intense, inner struggles, Abraham eventually accepted and then yielded to the Father's "sentence of death." Abraham did not fail in the bleakest hour of his life! He was willing to put his son to death as God had commanded and then trust God to raise Isaac from the dead.

God allowed Abraham to carry out His instructions up to the point where there could be no retreat—and then prevented him from laying a hand on his son. One could almost hear the Lord say, "It's all right, Abraham. I never planned for you to actually kill Isaac. I only wanted to remove from the throne of your heart any affection for your son that would come between you and Me. I needed to cut away any expectation or idea from your thinking that would later prevent both you and Isaac from fulfilling My destiny for your lives. It has all been necessary to keep the two of you from future pain and disillusionment!"

That day it was Abraham, not Isaac, who died! Abraham died to himself. He died to his own dreams and aspirations. Because Abraham did not withhold his son from the Lord, the heavens were opened to him! The "sentence of death" that Abraham chose to embrace became a door of hope and promise. In Genesis 22:17-18, God said, "blessing I will bless you, and multiplying I will multiply your descendants as the stars of the heaven, and as the sand which is on the seashore; and your descendants shall possess the gate of their enemies. In your seed all the nations of the earth shall be blessed, because you have obeyed My voice." God used the sentence of death to ultimately defeat death!

This same principle is further seen in the life and ministry of Jesus. Like Isaac:

Jesus was born of God and of promise,

46

He was the Anointed Son,
He was the hope of the future, and
He was to be the instrument of blessing to others.

Yet at thirty-three years of age and in the prime of His life, Jesus came under the Father's "sentence of death." In the Garden of Gethsemane, as He wrestled with the burden of what lay before Him, Jesus came to the place where He willingly surrendered to the process of death (Matthew 26:36-46).

According to Acts 2:25-28, Jesus was able to embrace the sentence of death because

1. He always beheld the Father (v.25),
2. He drew spiritual strength from knowing that the Father was always with Him (v.25),
3. He worshipped even as He went into death (v.26),
4. He maintained a living hope (v.26),
5. He knew life would come out of death (v.27), and
6. He experienced a satisfaction in the Father's presence (v.28).[1]

The death that Jesus endured was not a death without hope! Jesus never experienced decay; instead, He went through a metamorphosis process. Like a caterpillar transformed into a butterfly, the death of Christ brought with it newness of life. Again, God used death to defeat death! Even now, our heavenly Father is jealousy calling us to accept and embrace His "sentence of death." He is wanting to empty us of our own agendas so He alone can be Lord over our lives. He is seeking to remove from us every idea and opinion that would limit and control Him.

Are we willing to allow our dreams and expectations to die? This will be extremely difficult for us because we have come to believe that anything that has been born of God should live forever. Whether we are talking about personal ambitions and dreams or ministries and movements, the temptation will always be to try and keep alive what God is wanting to put to death. However, if we try to preserve what God wants to kill, it will end up producing nothing but death and decay!

Everything that is born of God must eventually come under the Father's "sentence of death!" If we resist this process, we will sabotage God's purpose for our lives. On the other hand, if we embrace death as Jesus did, we will experience a dimension of life that we never dreamed possible! Maybe this is what Oswald Chambers meant when he wrote, "This fundamental principle must be borne in mind, that any work for God before it fulfills its purpose must die, otherwise it 'abides alone.' The conception [idea] is not that of progress from seed to full growth, but of a seed dying and bringing forth what it never was."[2]

This is why it is vitally important that we

1. always behold the Father (look to Him and not our circumstances),
2. draw spiritual strength from always knowing that the Father is with us,
3. worship even as we go into death,
4. maintain a living hope,
5. believe life will come out of death, and
6. experience a satisfaction in the Father's presence (find our fulfillment in Him and nothing else).

Let us allow the Father to free us from anything that may be hiding behind our pain and disappointment. Let us ask Him to put His knife to the heart of our disillusionment, so we can be ushered into the destiny He has for each of us! Although His hands may wound, they also heal! His correction is never rejection! Even though we have fallen short on many occasions, He has never changed His mind concerning His purpose for our lives. This is why He brings us to the end of ourselves. He reduces us to nothing so He can make something new out of our lives. It is not a death without hope; it is a metamorphosis process. God is using death to defeat death! What stands before us is an open door into resurrection life. This is what revival is all about!

In his book *WINDOWS OF THE SOUL* Ken Gire shared the personal struggles he faced during a time of extreme change and transition. As he tried to understand what God was doing with his life, he went through periods of painful depression and disillusionment! Of his own spiritual pilgrimage he later wrote,

> Like the dark woods of a fairy tale, life too has its dark side. And somewhere down the road, if we travel long enough down that road, we will experience it. Who knows what woods that road will take us through or what frightening things may be crouching in their shadows?
>
> In the middle of my own journey I found myself in such a wood. The darkness of the woods was more terrifying than the starkness of the wilderness.
>
> It was for me a time of depression in which the trees were so dense and their shadows so long that I didn't know how to get out—or if I ever would get out. That was the fear. Not the darkness of the woods. Not the dangers in the shadows. But that the woods may never end.
>
> And so the sun went down and the woods got dark, and with the darkness came the tears. There I was, huddled in the rain, shivering, and the only thing I could do was pray for the dawn.
>
> I called out desperately to hear God during my long night in the woods. I called for direction, for understanding, for help. I asked for a way out, and if not a way out, at least a footprint letting me know He

was somewhere in the woods with me, a broken twig, something, anything. Had I been calling out too long or too loudly to hear His answer? I had certainly been lonely enough in my depression, but had I been attentive enough?

It was a day that lent itself to being attentive when I finally did hear something, or thought I did. It was a spring day. The day before, the temperature reached a high of eighty-three degrees. Today, though, there was six inches of snow. I walked in the backyard, stood, looked, listened.

A gesture of wind touched my face. The sound of a dog barking, sounding faraway but wasn't. The sound of faraway birds that weren't. The snow muffled everything, making everything seem distant, seeming as if the world had stepped back to give you room, to give you a space of your own where thoughts of your own could stretch and move around.

I looked around, slowly, not wanting to force anything or manipulate the moment in any way. And I saw plants pushing their way through the snow, struggling to be green, or so it seemed as I watched them. Two seasons were competing for the same ground. Spring struggling to be born. Winter struggling not to die. And it seemed to me some sort of parable. Was it a parable for me?

Then the husk of the parable opened up, revealing a kernel of truth. Something inside me was struggling to be born. Something else was struggling not to die. And they were both inside me at the same time, winter and spring, contesting each other. The ending of one was necessary for the beginning of the other."[3]

* Emphasis added

Chapter Four

FROM DESOLATION TO REVELATION

Oswald Chambers, the author of the widely read
devotional book, *MY UTMOST FOR HIS HIGH-
EST*, came to know the Lord as a young boy. He was
raised in a Christian home and grew up listening to
his father preach the Word of God in a Baptist
church in Aberdeen, Scotland.

He "enjoyed the presence of Jesus Christ wonderful-
ly," yet, according to his testimony, "years passed
before I gave myself up thoroughly to His work. I
was in Dunoon College as tutor of Philosophy when
Dr. F. B. Meyer came and spoke about the Holy
Spirit. I determined to have all that was going, and
went to my room and asked God simply and defi-
nitely for the baptism of the Holy Spirit, whatever
that meant.

From that day on for four years nothing but the over-
ruling grace of God and the kindness of friends kept
me out of an asylum. God used me during those
years for the conversion of souls, but I had no conscious communion with Him. The Bible was the
dullest, most uninteresting book in existence, and
the sense of depravity, the vileness and bad-motived-
ness of my nature was terrific. I see now that God

was taking me by the light of the Holy Spirit and His Word through every ramification of my being."

The last three months of those years things reached a climax. I was getting very desperate. I knew no one who had what I wanted. IN FACT, I DID NOT KNOW WHAT I DID WANT. BUT I KNEW THAT IF WHAT I HAD WAS ALL THE CHRIS-TIANITY THERE WAS, THE THING WAS A FRAUD. Then Luke 11:13 got hold of me, "If ye then, being evil, know how to give good gifts to your children, how much more shall your Heavenly Father give the Holy Spirit to them that ask Him?"

But how could I, bad-motived as I was, possibly ask for the gift of the Holy Spirit? Then it was borne in upon me that I had to claim the gift from God on the authority of Jesus Christ and testify to having done so. But the thought came—if you claim the gift of the Holy Spirit on the word of Jesus Christ and testify to it, God will make it known to those who know you best how bad you are in heart. And I was not willing to be a fool for Christ's sake. But those of you who know the experience, know very well how God brings one to the point of utter despair, and I got to the place where I did not care whether everyone knew how bad I was. I cared for nothing on earth, saving to get out of my present condition.

In a little meeting held during a Mission in Dunoon, a well-known lady was asked to take the after-meeting. She did not speak, but set us to prayer and then sang, "Touch Me Again, Lord." I felt nothing, but I knew emphatically my time had come, and I rose to my feet. I had no vision of God, only a sheer, dogged determination to take God at His Word and to prove this thing for myself. And I stood up and said so.

That was bad enough, but what followed was ten times worse. After I sat down, the speaker, who knew me well, said, "That is very good of our brother. He has spoken like that as an example to the rest of you."

Up I got again and said, "I got up for no one's sake. I got up for my own sake. Either Christianity is a downright fraud, or I have not got hold of the right end of the stick." And then, and there, I claimed the gift of the Holy Spirit in dogged committal on Luke 11:13. I had no vision of Heaven or of angels. I had nothing. I was as dry and empty as ever, no power or realization of God, no witness of the Holy Spirit.

Later I was asked to speak at a meeting, and forty souls came out to the front. Did I praise God? No, I was terrified and left them to the workers, and went to Mr. MacGregor and told him what had happened. He said, "Don't you remember claiming the Holy Spirit as a gift on the word of Jesus, and that He said, 'Ye shall receive power...'? This is the power from on high." And, like a flash, something happened inside me, and I saw that I had been wanting power in my hand, so to speak, that I might say, "Look what I have got by putting my all on the altar."

If the previous years had been Hell on earth, these four years have truly been Heaven on earth. Glory be to God, the last aching abyss of the human heart is filled to overflowing with the love of God. Love is the beginning, love is the middle, and love is the end. After He comes in, all you see is "Jesus only, Jesus ever."[1]

The spiritual crisis for Oswald Chambers had been worth all of his personal pain and confusion! Out of his own sense of barrenness and desperation, he had such an encounter with the Lord that it radically altered his life and made him into the man whose books are still read by tens of thousands around the world.

One does not have to study the subject of revival long before becoming aware of the fact that God always comes to His people when they reach the point of utter desperation! It was Jesus Himself who said, "Blessed are those who hunger and thirst for righteousness, For they shall be filled" (Matthew 5:6). There is an inevitable "spirit of desperation" that always accompanies hunger!

Several years ago, a soccer team was flying home from competition when their plane crashed in the Andes Mountains. Although many of the team members lost their lives in the accident, there were a handful of people who survived. After approximately nine days without food, those who were still alive began eating the frozen flesh of their deceased friends. They had been driven to do the unthinkable—all because of the "force of hunger."

Are we this desperate to experience personal revival? Smith Wigglesworth said, "To hunger and thirst after righteousness is when nothing in the world can fascinate us so much as being near to God."[2] Do we realize that we have as much of God as we have really wanted? God has never withheld Himself from the person who has longed for more of Him! Our problem is that we have settled for so little of God that we have become satisfied with other things!

A. W. Tozer once wrote, "The whole transaction of religious conversion has been made mechanical and spiritless....Christ may be 'received' without any special love for Him in the soul of the receiver. The man is 'saved,' but he is not hungry or thirsty after God. In fact, he is specifically taught to be satisfied and is encouraged to be content with little."[3]

Tozer also wrote,

> Suppose some angelic being who had since creation known the deep, still rapture of dwelling in the divine Presence would appear on earth and live awhile among us Christians. Don't you imagine he might be astonished at what he saw? He might, for instance, wonder how we can be contented with our poor, commonplace level of spiritual experience. In our hands, after all, is a message from God not only inviting us into His holy fellowship but also giving us detailed instructions about how to get there. After feasting on the bliss of intimate communion with God how could such a being understand the casual, easily satisfied spirit which characterizes most evangelicals today? And if our hypothetical being knew such blazing souls as Moses, David, Isaiah, Paul, John, Stephen, Augustine, Rolle, Rutherford, Newton, Brainerd and Faber, he might logically conclude that 20th century Christians had misunderstood some vital doctrine of the faith somewhere and had stopped short of true acquaintance with God.
>
> What if he sat in on the daily sessions of an average Bible conference and noted the extravagant claims we Christians make for ourselves as believers in Christ and compared them with our actual spiritual experiences? He would surely conclude that there

was a serious contradiction between what we think
we are and what we are in reality.[4]

It has been estimated that there are well over 300 million
"spirit-filled" believers alive in the world today. Yet if this is true,
how can the world still be in its present condition? There were 120
men and women filled with the Spirit on the Day of Pentecost, and
the shock waves released in the realm of the Spirit were soon felt
throughout their world!

Something is drastically wrong! How can so many believers
hear sermon after sermon and read book after book without experiencing any lasting change? It is time to be completely honest
with ourselves! We are not walking in the brand of Christianity
that once rocked the world! We have replaced the power of the
Gospel with programs, methods, organizations and a host of religious activities which now occupy our time and attention. The
great revivalist, Leonard Ravenhill, once said, "We [the Church]
have a lot of equipment, but not much enduement."

As long as we Christians continue to trust in religious organizations, material wealth, popular preaching and advertising cam-
paigns, we will never have revival! Samuel Chadwick was painfully correct when he wrote, "The Church always fails at the point of
self-confidence!"[5] When our confidence in the flesh finally shat-
ters and we come to the realization that our lives are truly barren
and desolate, then and only then will God break in and revive us!

Even now, the Spirit of God is bringing the Church to the point
of desperation! He is in the process of lovingly stripping us of our
unanointed activity and bringing us to the end of our strength. In
fact, He delights in reducing us to nothing! It is the "Law of
Genesis"—God always makes something out of nothing!

"Springs of former blessing" are also being allowed to dry up
(I Kings 17:1-24) in order for the "good" of God's provision to be
replaced by the "best" of His purposes! It is out of our dryness and

barrenness that God wants to give us new life! This can best be illustrated by a principle that is interwoven throughout the Word of God—**WHAT GOD BIRTHS, HE BIRTHS OUT OF BAR-RENNESS!** For example, Abraham's wife Sarah had been barren all of her life. According to Hebrews 11:11, Sarah eventually received the strength to conceive a child. Yet it was out of her barrenness that she not only gave birth to a son but also gave birth to an entire nation!

Some of the greatest leaders God ever raised up came from "barren" wombs. Men such as Isaac, Jacob, Joseph, Samson and John the Baptist were birthed out of barrenness!

Jesus Himself was even born out of barren conditions! The nation of Israel, just prior to the birth of Christ, was spiritually barren and dry. Biblical scholars believe that there had been no prophetic word for 400 years between the period of the Old and New Testaments. Yet it was out of this "climate" that the Son of God was born.

Isaac would grow up to become a "type" of Christ. Jacob would "wrestle with God" and prevail. Joseph would become the man who reunited the family of God. Samson would demonstrate the power of God to his generation. John the Baptist would become the prophetic voice who ushered in the First Coming of Christ. And Jesus became the "root out of dry [barren] ground" (Isaiah 53:2). Ministry was birthed out of barrenness! When we see what God did through the lives of these individuals, we cannot help but take heart!

This principle can be further reinforced by looking at the life of Moses. Although Moses was not born out of a barren womb, he found himself having to endure a long season of incredible desolation.

Out of his own zeal and sense of destiny, Moses had tried, but failed, to deliver the children of Israel from the tyranny of Egypt.

He was rejected by his own people and wanted as a fugitive by Pharaoh. Moses was forced to flee for his life and lived in desolation for 40 years! The barrenness of his surroundings accurately reflected the barrenness of his own life!

It was toward the end of this 40 year period that Moses "...led the flock [of Jethro] to the back of the desert, and came to Horeb, the mountain of God" (Exodus 3:1). The word "Horeb" in the Hebrew means "desolation." From this place of desolation, Moses was given a fresh revelation of God (the Lord appeared to Moses in the burning bush), as well as a new beginning. God used Moses' season of barrenness to prepare him for a new anointing and ministry. Moses was taken from "desolation" to "revelation," and out of his barrenness a ministry was birthed that impacted a nation!

We also see this same principle in the life of Elijah. After battling and overcoming the prophets of Baal on the heights of Mount Carmel, Elijah found himself in a valley of discouragement. Feeling as though he had stood alone in championing the Lord's cause, he fled from Jezebel until he was completely exhausted. Despondent and discouraged, he sat beneath a broom tree in the wilderness and prayed that he would die, saying, "...It is enough! Now, Lord, take my life, for I am no better than my fathers!" (I Kings 19:4).

Elijah then lay down and slept. "Suddenly an angel touched him, and said to him, 'Arise and eat.' Then he looked, and there by his head was a cake baked on coals, and a jar of water. So he ate and drank, and lay down again. And the angel of the Lord came back the second time, and touched him, and said, 'Arise and eat, because the journey is too great for you.' So he arose, and ate and drank; and he went in the strength of that food forty days and forty nights..." (I Kings 19:5-8).

The Lord then led Elijah, as He had led Moses, to Horeb, the "place of desolation." Alone and dejected, Elijah retreated into a cave on the side of the mountain. Yet it was here that he was given a fresh revelation of the God he served.

Throughout his ministry, Elijah had experienced mighty manifestations of the Spirit. Yet when God came to him on Mount Horeb, it was not in the earthquake, the fire or the storm. The Lord spoke to him in a still, small voice (I Kings 19:11-12). Elijah encountered the whisper of God and the wind of His presence in a way he never had before!

During this time of quiet solitude, the Lord also brought a new beginning to Elijah's life, one that would ultimately usher in a "double portion" of power and anointing to be passed on to his servant Elisha! Through this new anointing, Jezebel would be destroyed and Baal worship annihilated. God took Elijah from a "place of desolation" into a realm of new revelation and birthed a ministry which included twice as many miracles.

Today the Spirit of God is calling us out of barrenness and desolation into new life and ministry! God's promise to us is that we, too, will receive a "double portion" (Isaiah 61:7; John 14:12). He is wanting to birth "spiritual Isaacs" who will manifest the life and character of Christ. He is seeking to empower a people who, like Jacob, will wrestle with Him in prayer—and prevail. Even now, He is in the process of raising up a "Joseph Company" who will carry the burden for restoring the family of God.

Out of holy jealousy for His Son, the Father is going to have a people who, like Samson, will demonstrate His power to their generation and who, like Moses, will behold His glory and know of His ways. He is going to release into the world a "John the Baptist-type ministry " which will usher in the Second Coming of Christ.

The first "law of ministry," however, is acknowledging our own spiritual barrenness. We can do nothing on our own; God is the only One who can create life! How desperate are we? It was

Rachel who, out of her barrenness, cried to her husband, "...Give me children, or else I die" (Genesis 30:1). Only then did she conceive! What is the cry of our hearts? How badly do we want our Bridegroom, the Lord Jesus, to come and impregnate us with His Life?

God longs to come to us! He wants to give us a fresh revelation of Himself! As Charles Finney once said, "God is One pent-up Revival!" It is within His nature to want to revive us. What are we waiting for? Let us release the cry of our hearts! Let us admit to our spiritual need! Let us ask the Holy Spirit to create within us a "vacuum of desire" into which He can rush!

In his book *BORN AFTER MIDNIGHT*, A. W. Tozer wrote,

> Hunger and thirst are physical sensations which, in their acute stages, may become real pain. It has been the experience of countless seekers after God that when their desires became a pain they were suddenly and wonderfully filled. The problem is not to persuade God to fill us, but to want God sufficiently to permit Him to do so. The average Christian is so cold and so contented with His wretched condition that there is no vacuum of desire into which the blessed Spirit can rush in satisfying fullness.

> Occasionally there will appear on the religious scene a man whose unsatisfied spiritual longings become so big and important in his life that they crowd out every other interest. Such a man refuses to be content with the safe and conventional prayers of the frost-bound brethren who "lead in prayer" week after week and year after year in the local assemblies. His yearnings carry him away and often make something of a nuisance out of him. His puzzled fellow Christians shake their heads and look knowing-

ly at each other, but like the blind man who cried after his sight and was rebuked by the disciples, he "cries the more a great deal." And if he has not yet met the conditions or there is something hindering the answer to his prayer, he may pray on in the late hours. Not the hour of night but the state of his heart decides the time of his visitation.[9]

The story is told of a young man who, in his search for God, came to study at the feet of an old wise man. One day the teacher took his pupil to a lake and led him out into shoulder-deep water. Placing his hands on the student's head, he suddenly pushed him underwater and held him there until the young man, in desperation, fought his way to the surface. In utter shock and confusion, the student stared at the old man as if to ask, "What in the world are you doing?" The teacher, in response, looked at his pupil and said, "When you want God as much as you wanted air, you shall find Him."

REVIVE THY WORK, O LORD

Revive Thy work, O Lord!
Thy mighty arm make bare;
Speak with the voice that wakes the dead,
And make Thy people hear!
Revive Thy work, O Lord!
Disturb this sleep of death;
Quicken the smould'ring embers now
By Thine Almighty breath.

Revive Thy work, O Lord!
Create soul-thirst for Thee;
And hung'ring for the bread of life,
Oh, may our spirits be!
Revive Thy work, O Lord!
Exalt Thy precious name;
And by the Holy Ghost, our love
For Thee and Thine inflame.

Revive Thy work, O Lord,
While here to Thee we bow;
Descend, O gracious Lord, descend,
O, come and bless us now!

Fanny J. Crosby

Chapter Five

THE BUILDING OF ANOINTED MINISTRY

On a dirt road in the middle of a wide field stood a beautiful carriage, something on the order of a stagecoach, but all edged in gold, and with beautiful carvings. It was pulled by six large chestnut horses, two in the lead, two in the middle, and two in the rear. But they were not moving, they were not pulling the carriage, and I wondered why. Then I saw the driver underneath the carriage, on the ground on his back, just behind the last two horses' heels, working on something between the front wheels of the carriage. I thought, "My, he is in a dangerous place; for if one of those horses kicked or stepped back, they could kill him, or if they decided to go forward, or got frightened somehow, they would pull the carriage right over him." But he didn't seem afraid, for he knew that those horses were disciplined and would not move till he told them to move. The horses were not stamping their feet nor acting restless, and though there were bells on their feet, the bells were not tinkling. There were pom-poms on their harness over their heads, but the pom-poms were not moving. They were simply standing still and quiet, waiting for the voice of the Master.

As I watched the harnessed horses, I noticed two young colts coming out of the open field, and they approached the carriage and seemed to say to the horses: "Come and play with us, we have many fine games, we will race with you, come catch us..." And with that the colts kicked up their heels, flicked their tails and raced across the open field. But when they looked back and saw the horses were not following, they were puzzled. They knew nothing of the harnesses, and could not understand why the horses did not want to play. So they called to them: "Why do you not race with us? Are you tired? Are you too weak? Do you not have strength to run? You are much too solemn, you need more joy in life." But the horses answered not a word, nor did they stamp their feet or toss their heads. But they stood, quiet and still, waiting for the voice of the Master.

Again the colts called to them: "Why do you stand so in the hot sun? Come over here in the shade of this nice tree. See how green the grass is? You must be hungry, come and feed with us, it is so green and so good. You look thirsty, come drink of one of our many streams of cool clear water." But the horses answered them with not so much as a glance, but stood still, waiting for the command to go forward with the King. And then the scene changed, and I saw lariat nooses fall around the necks of the two colts, and they were led off to the Master's corral for training [breaking] and discipline. How sad they were as the lovely green fields disappeared, and they were put into the confinement of the Corral with its brown dirt and high fence. The colts ran from fence to fence, seeking freedom, but found that they were confined to this place of training.

And then the Trainer began to work on them, with his Whip and His Bridle. What a death for those who had been all their lives accustomed to such a freedom! They could not understand the reason for this torture, this terrible discipline. What crime had they done to deserve this? Little did they know of the responsibility that was to be theirs when they had submitted to the discipline, learned to perfectly obey the Master, and finished their training. All they knew was that this processing was the most horrible thing they had ever known.

One of the colts rebelled under the training, and said, "This is not for me. I like my freedom, my green hills, my flowing streams of fresh water. I will not take any more of this confinement, this terrible training." So he found a way out, jumped the fence and ran happily back to the meadows of grass. And I was astonished that the Master let him go, and went not after him. But He devoted His attention to the remaining colt. This colt, though he had the same opportunity to escape, decided to submit his own will, and learn the ways of the Master. And the training got harder than ever, but he was rapidly learning more and more how to obey the slightest wish of the Master, and to respond to even the quietness of His voice. And I saw that had there been no training, no testing, there would have been neither submission nor rebellion from either of the colts. For in the field they did not have the choice to rebel or submit, they were sinless in their innocence. But when brought to the place of testing and training and discipline, then was made manifest the obedience of one and the rebellion of the other. And though it seemed safer not to come to the place of discipline because of the risk of being found rebellious, yet I saw that without this there could be no sharing of His glory, no Sonship.

Finally this period of training was over. Was he now rewarded with his freedom, and sent back to the fields? Oh no. But a greater confinement than ever now took place, as a harness dropped about his shoulders. Now he found there was not even the freedom to run about the small corral, for in the harness he could only move where and when His Master spoke. And unless the Master spoke, he stood still.

The scene changed, and I saw the other colt standing on the side of a hill, nibbling at some grass. Then across the fields, down the road came the King's carriage, drawn by six horses. With amazement he saw that in the lead, on the right side, was his brother colt, now made strong and mature on the good corn in the Master's stable. He saw the lovely pom-poms shaking in the wind, noticed the glittering gold bordered harness about his brother, heard the beautiful tinkling of the bells on his feet...and envy came into his heart. Thus he complained to himself: "Why has my brother been so honored, and I am neglected? They have not put bells on MY feet, nor pom-poms on MY head. The Master has not given ME the wonderful responsibility of pulling His carriage, nor put about me the golden harness. Why have they chosen my brother instead of me?" And by the Spirit the answer came back to me as I watched. "Because one submitted to the will and discipline of the Master, and one rebelled, thus has one been chosen and the other set aside."

Then I saw a great drought sweep across the coun-
tryside, and the green grass became dead, dry,
brown and brittle. The little streams of water dried
up, stopped flowing, and there was only a small
muddy puddle here and there. I saw the little colt (I
was amazed that it never seemed to grow or mature)
as he ran here and there, across the fields looking
for fresh streams and green pastures, finding none.
Still he ran, seemingly in circles, always looking for
something to feed his famished spirit. But there
was a famine in the land, and the rich green pastures
and flowing streams of yesterday were not to be
had. And one day the colt stood on the hillside on
weak and wobbly legs, wondering where to go next
to find food, and how to get strength to go. Seemed
like there was no use, for good food and flowing
streams were a thing of the past, and all the efforts
to find more only taxed his waning strength.
Suddenly he saw the King's carriage coming down
the road, pulled by six great horses. And he saw his
brother, fat and strong, muscles rippling, sleek and
beautiful with much grooming. His heart was
amazed and perplexed, and he cried out: "My brother, where do you find the food to keep you strong
and fat in these days of famine? I have run everywhere in my freedom, searching for food, and I find
none. Where do you, in your awful confinement,
find food in this time of drought? Tell me, please,
for I must know!" And then the answer came back
from a voice filled with victory and praise: "In my
Master's House, there is a secret place in the con-

fining limitations of His stables where He feeds me by His own hand, and His granaries never run empty, and His well never runs dry." And with that the Lord made me to know that in the day when people are weak and famished in their spirits in the time of spiritual famine, that those who have lost their own wills, and have come into the secret place of the most High, into the utter confinement of His perfect will, shall have plenty of the corn of Heaven, and a never ending flow of fresh streams of revelation by His Spirit.[1]

Although this vision was given by the Spirit to an individual many years ago, its message is still relevant for those of us who long for personal revival! The human heart is much like the untamed colt with its unbridled energy. At times it can be vibrant and majestic, yet it can also be obstinate and rebellious. In spite of its potential, the untamed heart has limited capacity for any real use. Just as an unbroken horse cannot be ridden for enjoyment or used for constructive work, a person with an unbroken spirit will never experience his true potential.

Let us notice, as well, that while the wild colt in the vision avoided the bit and bridle, it looked in envy at the smooth gait of the other horses. It longed for the care and affection given to the harnessed horses but opposed the process needed to achieve that honor.

The human heart can also be wildly undisciplined! At times it runs from God's harnessing like the wild colt and balks at the training of the Master. Although it seeks success and fulfillment, it is inevitably destined to a life of futility because of an unwillingness to completely surrender to the desires of the King.

This chapter discusses the taming of the human heart. We are going to discover that there is an active process in the building of Christian character called brokenness. Just as God births life out of barrenness, He also **BUILDS ANOINTED MINISTRY OUT OF BROKENNESS**. No one who has experienced personal revival or been used significantly by the Lord has ever escaped this process!

We can understand this principle even more clearly by studying two parallels between the taming of a horse and the breaking of a human heart. We can observe that the breaking process strengthens the bond between a trainer (owner, rider) and a horse. The love relationship is able to mature as trust is developed. Similarly, until a person is broken by the Lord, their relationship tends to be shallow and sporadic at best.

Secondly, one would think that the breaking process would drain the spirit and energy of a horse. However, a horse is actually just as strong after breaking as before, yet his resourcefulness is multiplied many times over, and his energy is no longer wild, but focused. As far as the human spirit is concerned, the process of brokenness is never meant to cause anyone to become indifferent and unmotivated. Instead, it is to be a catalyst which will ultimately help him reach his true potential in Christ!

THE NATURE OF BROKENNESS

What do we mean, then, when we talk about being broken by the Lord? One of the best definitions for the word "broken" found in the dictionary is "to be tamed." In the Hebrew language, the word "broken" literally means to "splinter into pieces." However, throughout the Old Testament other words are also used to illustrate the concept, each with its distinct shade of meaning. For example, the word that is used to describe a broken heart can also

71

be translated "shattered." It is used this way in Jeremiah 2:13 in the picturesque phrase "broken cisterns, that can hold no water." It is also mentioned in Ezekiel 27:34 to describe the breaking up of a ship caught in the middle of a storm and in Ezekiel 34:4 to speak of a sheep that has fallen from a height and has suffered broken bones. In Daniel 8:22 this word is again used to describe the rough goat's horn that was broken off by its adversary.

These word pictures reinforce the real essence of brokenness. When the writers of the Scriptures used the word to describe a human heart, they referred to a heart which, through crisis or process, had been shattered to pieces. What formerly was hard and stubborn had become compliant and pliable.

A broken person is like the shattered cistern—empty of his own resources. Like the ocean-going vessel torn apart by the rough and turbulent seas, the broken heart is shipwrecked on God. A broken individual is like a sheep, wounded through its own wanderings and lying at the feet of the good Shepherd. The soul that is broken is like the animal of Daniel's vision, stripped of its former power and might and now submissive before Almighty God.

The idea of "pruning" mentioned by Jesus in John 15 is another biblical analogy for the process of brokenness. Our heavenly Father is referred to as the Vinedresser who prunes His vines. While pruning may seem illogical, fruit growers understand that vines or trees which are "cut back" will give a better quality of fruit! The process of "pruning" describes God's activity in our lives, while brokenness points to the intended result in our hearts. Jesus clearly indicated that everyone would be "cut back" at times, some for their lack of fruitfulness and others for increased fruitfulness. No true believer can ever avoid the process!

Another concept in Scripture similar to brokenness is the call to absolute surrender. This type of surrender involves relinquishing all rights to the control of our own lives and, in humility, allowing

King Jesus to reign supreme. Human nature despises the thought of surrendering because it hates being controlled, even by God Himself. Yet, the Lord cannot use us in any significant way until we take our hands off and lay our lives down at His feet. When we "give up" and surrender our wills completely to Him, then we truly become His!

While the terms "broken" and "broken-hearted" do not occur frequently in the Bible, the concept of brokenness is also symbolized by such words as "contrite," "humble" and "poor." Brokenness is really nothing more than an attitude of heart in which an individual takes his place before God in humility, confessing his absolute, continual need of divine grace and assistance. Brokenness enables us to realize where we would be apart from the favor of the Lord.

A broken heart is a yielded heart, completely open before the Lord and empty of pride and self-will. In brokenness we discover that we are poor and needy when originally we thought we were rich and in need of nothing. The Greek word for "poor" mentioned in the New Testament literally means "to cower" or "cringe" and refers to the beggarly and desperately poor. When we are "poor in spirit," we come to God crying out for him to sustain us. We come to Him on His terms with a heart of gratitude because we do not deserve anything we have or will ever receive. Being poor in spirit means being aware of our own spiritual inadequacies; it means recognizing the fact that in the Kingdom of God filing for "spiritual bankruptcy," rather than the end, is really just the beginning of spiritual breakthrough.

THE NECESSITY OF BROKENNESS

From a scriptural standpoint, there can be no doubt that brokenness is to be viewed as the one essential condition of heart for God to respond to us in our time of need. Norman Grubb, a missionary and author of several well-known books, went so far as to suggest that "brokenness" is the key word for continuous revival![2] If we are to be revived and transformed, the Lord requires that we come before Him with broken hearts and contrite spirits.

In Psalm 34:18, we read, "The Lord is near to those who have a broken heart, And saves such as have a contrite spirit." In this passage brokenness is seen as the necessary stipulation for God's presence to come to us in renewed power and strength. The Lord always rushes to the rescue of the brokenhearted.

Psalm 51:17 states that "The sacrifices of God are a broken spirit, A broken and a contrite heart—These, O God, You will not despise." According to King David, brokenness is a primary requirement for God's acceptance and favor. The Psalmist realized from his own personal sin and failure that God took no delight in burnt offerings that were not accompanied by a heart of repentance. It is the broken heart that brings with it a heightened sensitivity toward sin.

Why has revival tarried? The Lord promised in Isaiah 57:15 that He would "...dwell...With him who has a contrite and humble spirit, To revive the spirit of the humble, And to revive the heart of the contrite ones." This verse specifically teaches that brokenness is a key ingredient in revival! Consequently, we do not need to look any further to explain the lack of genuine revival among many Christians today. Brokenness is an aspect of Christian experience that has been sadly overlooked even in the current emphasis upon spiritual renewal. While there has been much human brilliance displayed within the Church over the years, there has been far too little true brokenness expressed. God's manifest presence cannot be continually experienced in and through individuals whose hearts are not broken before Him.

In Isaiah 66:2, God said, "...on this one will I look: On him who is poor and of a contrite spirit, And who trembles at My word."

Brokenness is again seen as a critical requirement for the Lord's special favor and blessing. God "looks" in the direction of the one with a broken heart.

Brokenness is also beautifully portrayed in Mark 14:3-9, in which the story is told of a woman who came to Jesus with a flask of very expensive perfume. As the jar was broken and the perfume was poured on the head of the Son of God, John 12 tells us that "...the house was filled with the fragrance of the oil" (John 12:3). The aroma of the costly oil would not have been released if the alabaster flask had not been broken!

Paul wrote in 2 Corinthians 4:7, "But we have this treasure in earthen vessels, that the excellence of the power may be of God and not of us." Jesus, the Treasure, is contained in the vessels of our lives. Yet, if our lives are not broken, who will be able to discover the Treasure within? It is only as our earthen vessels are shattered that the life and aroma of Christ can be released!

The necessity of brokenness is even illustrated for us in nature. Jesus said in John 12:24, "...unless a grain of wheat falls into the ground and dies, it remains alone; but if it dies, it produces much grain." It is important to note that the life is in the grain of wheat, yet as long as the outward shell remains unbroken, the wheat cannot sprout and grow. However, once the shell is broken, it becomes the very fertilizer for its own new shoot. The fruit grows as the seed dies!

What, then, is the ultimate purpose of the Spirit's working in our lives? It is to break open the alabaster box of our lives; it is to shatter our earthen vessels; it is to crack open the shell of our hearts so He can touch the world through those of us who belong to Him. Brokenness is the way of fragrance, the way of fruitfulness and the way of blessing!

PRODUCT-ORIENTED VS. PROCESS-ORIENTED

We, in Western civilization, are product-oriented people. We read self-help books to try and increase our productivity. Our natural tendency is to do more in order to achieve more. God, on the other hand, is process-oriented. While we gather information on how to bear fruit as Christians, our heavenly Father is calling us to yield to His work in our lives so that we can truly be productive.

In an orchard, the trees do not groan and strain to bear fruit! Producing fruit comes naturally as the branches draw their nourishment from the tree. In contrast, we Christians tend to try to work to produce fruit. Yet what we must realize is that the more we abide in Christ and yield to His activity in our lives, the more we will automatically bear the fruit of His Spirit. Brokenness is a divine activity that God uses to make us more fruitful. It is a part of the process that not only produces true Christian character but also builds true **anointed** ministry.

None of us is equipped for godly service simply because we have acquired a knowledge of the Scriptures, earned a degree or learned some new method or technique. It is sad that some still believe that if they can only assimilate more teaching, they will somehow be fit for ministry. The real issue in our lives, however, is not only one of information but also radical transformation. What kind of men and women are we? How can an individual whose doctrine is right but whose life is not being conformed to the character of Christ ever expect to impact the Church, let alone the world?

What, then, is the intention of our heavenly Father as He leads us in the way of brokenness? John the Baptist put it best when he said, "He [Jesus] must increase, but I must decrease" (John 3:30). It is the realization that, apart from Christ, we can do nothing that has any eternal value (John 15:5)! For us, it is becoming less so that

He can become more. Samuel Logan Brengle, a leader of the Salvation Army, was once introduced as "the great Dr. Brengle." That same day, Brengle wrote in his diary, "If I appear great in their eyes, the Lord is most graciously helping me to see how absolutely nothing I am without Him, and helping me to keep little in my eyes. He does use me. But I am so concerned that He uses me and that it is not of me the work is done. The axe cannot boast of the trees it has cut down. It could do nothing but for the woodsman. The moment he throws it aside, it becomes only old iron. O that I may never lose sight of this."[3]

In Revelation 3:17, Jesus addressed a church which had become all too self-sufficient. "Because you say, 'I am rich, have become wealthy, and have need of nothing'—and do not know that you are wretched, miserable, poor, blind, and naked...'" The charge is even more intriguing when you realize that this church was located in the city of Laodicea, which was the center for banking, for special eye ointment and for clothing. These individuals prided themselves in their achievements, but Jesus told them their self-sufficiency meant nothing!

Our self-sufficient culture is one of the biggest obstacles preventing us from experiencing the power and presence of God! We are inundated with ideologies that promote self-esteem, self-confidence, self-assertion and self-realization. What a contrast to the life and ministry of Christ! Jesus said, "Take My yoke upon you and learn from Me, for I am gentle and lowly in heart..." (Matthew 11:29). From the Gospel of John we hear Him echo this same theme: "...the Son can do nothing of Himself..." (5:19); "I can of Myself do nothing...I do not seek My own will..." (5:30); "I do not receive honor from men" (5:41); "...I have come down from heaven, not to do My own will..." (6:38); "...I have not come of Myself..." (7:28); "...I do nothing of Myself..." (8:28); "...I do not seek My own glory..." (8:50). Jesus' life continually illustrated His utter dependence upon the Father.

It was R. A. Torrey, an English preacher, who once said, "Oh, how many a man has been full of promise and God has used him, and then that man thought that he was the whole thing and God was compelled to set him aside! I believe more promising workers have gone on the rocks through self-sufficiency and self-esteem than through any other cause."[4]

In our day, we also need to learn the lessons of brokenness. Each of us must allow the Lord to bring us to the place where we embrace the "weakness" that accompanies the breaking process. We must realize that more people have failed in time of "strength" than in time of "weakness." This was vividly illustrated in the life of King Uzziah. According to 2 Chronicles 26:5, "...as long as he sought the Lord, God made him prosper." "But when he was **strong** his heart was lifted up, to his destruction, for he transgressed against the Lord his God by entering the temple of the Lord to burn incense on the altar of incense" (v.16).*

This truth was also lived out in the life of King Saul. In 1 Samuel 15:17 we find a perfect example of the "weakness of strength." After Saul repeatedly sinned against the Lord, Samuel the prophet was sent to him with a very revealing word. Samuel said, "...When you were **little** in your own eyes, were you not head of the tribes of Israel? And did not the Lord anoint you king over Israel?...Because you have rejected the word of the Lord, He also has rejected you from being king" (vs.17,23).*

Our hearts are never more unguarded than in times of blessing and prosperity! While each of us would love to enjoy lives of uninterrupted success, during such times it is far too easy to spiritually relax and rely upon our own strengths and abilities. It was this very tendency that motivated the Lord to say to the children of Israel, "When you have eaten and are full, then you shall bless the Lord your God for the good land which He has given you. Beware that you do not forget the Lord your God by not keeping His commandments, His judgments, and His statutes which I command you today, lest—when you have eaten and are full, and have built beautiful houses and dwell in them; and when your herds and your flocks multiply, and your silver and your gold are multiplied, and all that you have is multiplied; when your heart is lifted up, and you forget the Lord your God who brought you out of the land of Egypt, from the house of bondage;...then you say in your heart, 'My power and the might of my hand have gained me this wealth'"(Deuteronomy 8:10-14,17).

One of the greatest sins we can commit is the sin of a self-run life. The will to run one's own life and depend upon one's own strength probably destroys more people than anything else! God must use the "way of weakness" in our lives to guard against this very tendency.

There is a "strength in weakness" that God clearly seeks to develop in every one of us. This has always been His method of preparing a people to fulfill His purposes in the earth. When Israel, after crossing the Red Sea, failed to enter the Land of Canaan because of unbelief, God raised up a new generation under new leadership to embrace what He had promised them. Yet before they could obtain their inheritance, they were given detailed instructions in preparation for the conquering of Canaan.

This new generation had not been circumcised in the desert, and they still carried the "reproach of Egypt" with them. The very memory of the old life in Egypt had to be removed! What did God do with this nation He was preparing to use in battle against His enemies? Did He have them circumcised on the eastern bank of the Jordan River so they would have adequate time to recover before they fought the Canaanites? If that had happened, the Israelites at least would have had the added protection of high waters, because the Jordan was flooding her banks at that time of the year. Instead, God led His people across the river and totally crippled the sons of Israel right under the noses of the mighty men of Jericho. He weakened them in the presence of their enemies!

No doubt the hearts of the people must have melted as they watched many of their young men incapacitated in one sudden stroke at the command of God. Yet at the very time God was "weakening" His army, the hearts of the enemies of Israel "melted" and "...there was no more spirit [courage] in them any longer because of the children of Israel" (Joshua 5:1). It was the obedience of God's people and their identification with the "way of weakness" that brought dread and terror to the enemies of the Lord!

We can see this same pattern acted out time and again throughout the pages of Scripture. In Judges 3:15, we are introduced to a man named Ehud. Ehud was a Benjamite whom God raised up to save Israel out of the hands of Eglon, the king of Moab. The interesting thing about Ehud was that he was a left-handed judge.

Why would the Holy Spirit appear to go out of His way to record such a seemingly insignificant detail? The answer can be found in the name of the tribe from which Ehud came. The name "Benjamin" in the Hebrew language means "son of my right hand." The right hand in Scripture always symbolizes strength. In contrast, the left hand always depicts weakness. God used a left-handed judge from the tribe of Benjamin to put an end to the oppression of wicked King Eglon. With one thrust of a two-edged dagger by a "man of weakness," deliverance came to an entire nation (v.21)!

In the sixth chapter of Judges, we find the nation of Israel suffering terrible oppression at the hands of the Midianites. The people cried out to God for deliverance, and in answer to their pleas, the Lord raised up a man named Gideon. Gideon had been threshing grain by the winepress in order to hide it from the Midianites (v.11). When the Angel of the Lord appeared to Gideon, He greeted him with these strange words: "The Lord is with you, you mighty man of valor" (v.12). God knew Gideon's problem; He understood that Gideon was filled with fear because of the brutality of the enemy. He recognized that he was a poor man in one of the poorest families in Manasseh. The Lord also knew that Gideon was the least in his father's house. Yet, these were the very qualities God was looking for! The Lord then said to him, "...Go in this might of yours, and you shall save Israel from the hand of the Midianites..." (v.14). Gideon's strength was not to be found in his own resources, but in the acknowledgment of his weakness. The fact that God sent him would be the only authority he needed!

God then reduced the original army of 32,000 men to a mere handful. Gideon demobilized his army at the command of the Lord, until there were just 10,000 left. Although the men remaining were all anxious for battle, the Lord said, "...The people are still too many..." (Judges 7:4). God took matters into His own hands and sent another 9,700 home. In the end, only 300 men were chosen, not to display their might or strength but to demonstrate that in the weakness of man, God would be honored and exalted! With nothing more than torches, pitchers and trumpets, the army of Israel went forth to battle! This was all they needed because the battle was the Lord's.

Torches in pitchers? Trumpets? What odd instruments of war! Yet as the pitchers were broken and the trumpets were blown, the light within the pitchers was seen by everyone, and the Word of God resounded throughout the land—"The sword of the Lord and of Gideon" (Judges 7:20). The enemies of God were overwhelmed; they scattered in utter confusion! What an outstanding victory! Yet this is always God's battle strategy! The forces of darkness will always tremble when they see a people walking in the way of weakness—the way of brokenness!

This principle is further reinforced through the pen of the Apostle Paul: "But God has chosen the foolish things of the world to put to shame the wise, and God has chosen the weak things of the world to put to shame the things which are mighty" (1 Corinthians 1:27). When are we going to learn that the way up is the way down (James 4:10) and that "...the Spirit also helps in our weaknesses" (Romans 8:26)? He does not join Himself to our strengths or natural abilities. He links Himself to our weaknesses. This is what makes us strong—strong in the Lord!

Paul understood this truth in a way very few men ever have! In 2 Corinthians 11:23-28, he lists his ministerial credentials. "Are they ministers of Christ?—I speak as a fool—I am more: in labors more abundant, in stripes above measure, in prisons more frequently, in deaths often. From the Jews five times I received forty stripes minus one. Three times I was beaten with rods; once I was stoned; three times I was shipwrecked; a night and a day I have been in the deep; in journeys often, in perils of waters, in perils of robbers, in perils of my own countrymen, in perils of the Gentiles, in perils in the city, in perils in the wilderness, in perils in the sea, in perils among false brethren; in weariness and toil, in sleeplessness often, in hunger and thirst, in fastings often, in cold and nakedness—besides the other things, what comes upon me daily: my deep concern for all the churches."

Circumstances hemmed Paul in on all sides. His path of escape was completely cut off. His trust in his own abilities was entirely broken! Paul was even puzzled over God's dealings in his life and mystified over unrepeatable revelations, unalleviated suffering and unanswered pleas. Yet through it all, God was making Paul weak enough to be mighty! This is the law of brokenness!

When God wants to drill a man
And thrill a man
And skill a man,
When God wants to mold a man
To play the noblest part;
When He yearns with all His heart
To create so great and bold a man
That all the world shall be amazed,
Watch His methods, watch his ways!
How He ruthlessly perfects
Whom He royally elects!
How He hammers him and hurts him,
And with mighty blows converts him
Into trial shapes of clay which
Only God understands;
While his tortured heart is crying
And he lifts beseeching hands!
How He bends but never breaks
When his good He undertakes;
And with every purpose fuses him;
By every act induces him
To try His splendor out —
God knows what He's about!

Author Unknown

Chapter Six

LIVES UNDER CONSTRUCTION

THE PROCESS OF BROKENNESS

Although brokenness can be experienced during times of seeking the Lord and close encounters with Him (Isaiah 6:1-8; Genesis 32:24-32), it is more often than not produced during seasons of personal failure (2 Samuel 11; Psalm 51), setbacks and unexpected hardship (Job 1-2). Brokenness also comes in the form of personal betrayal, criticism and rejection. Life's upheavals can occur in a sudden, dramatic fashion, or they can take place through the gradual deterioration of our circumstances. Regardless of the "packages" in which they come, our response to the Lord during such times is the all-important issue!

Our concepts of success and the Christian life often prevent us from properly coping with difficulty. Trials and adversity just do not fit into our nice neat formulas for spiritual success. We can understand why bad things happen to bad people, but somehow we have come to believe that only good things should happen to good people! This is why we often do not deal well with turmoil and pain. We complain, get depressed, and at times, even resent the fact that God allowed the problems in the first place. We find ourselves tempted to retreat into various forms of escape—television, entertainment, alcohol, over-eating, pornography—in order to avoid dealing with the pressures of the moment!

Adversity and pain, however, are primary ingredients in the process of brokenness. When a sculptor creates a work of beauty from a marble slab, he does not use scissors or tweezers to form its shape; hammer and chisel are necessary if the marble is to become anything more than a colorful yet formless stone.

When God forms human character, He cuts deeply! He lovingly chisels away anything that would detract from our being formed into His likeness.

A sculptor once began to fashion a horse out of a large block of marble. Out of curiosity a bystander asked him, "How are you able to do this?" "Simple," the sculptor replied. "I just start chipping away, and I chip away anything that does not look like a horse."

So often we focus on the situations that surround us instead of seeing the loving hands of the Sculptor at work in our lives. We want our circumstances to change more than we are willing to allow the Lord to change our hearts. We play the blame game! We blame the conditions that threaten us or the people who have rejected us—we even blame God!

Yet the Scripture is clear: "Every good gift and every perfect gift is from above, and comes down from the Father of lights, with whom there is no variation or shadow of turning" (James 1:17). God does not do bad things to people! When allowing adversity into our lives, He is not getting even with us because of past mistakes! The love of our Father is so awesome that when "junk" does happen to us, He is always looking for a way to recycle our trash! He wants to retrieve "gold" out of our "garbage." This is the heart of Romans 8:28: "...all things [ultimately] work together for good to those who love God, to those who are the called according to His purpose."

God is in control of every aspect of our lives. Nothing can touch us without first passing through His hands (Job 2:1-7). The trials and tests are meant to promote us, not overwhelm us. Even the correction He brings to our lives because of our own failings is

86

His way of preparing us for something better. The extraordinary plans He has for each of us always require extraordinary preparation!

What ultimately matters is our attitude toward the difficulties we face. This is what the Apostle Paul came to realize through the grace of God. In 2 Corinthians 12:10, he was able to say "...I take pleasure in infirmities [weaknesses], in reproaches, in needs, in persecutions, in distresses, for Christ's sake. For when I am weak, then I am strong." Paul faced things that could easily have overcome him, yet he delighted in them! He went from "buffeting" to "boasting," from "sighing" to "singing!"

James 1:2-4 says, "My brethren, count it all joy when you fall into various trials, knowing that the testing of your faith produces patience [endurance]. But let patience [endurance] have its perfect work, that you may be perfect [mature] and complete, lacking nothing." James is not telling us to "fake it" in times of hardship and pain. Instead, he is instructing us to change our outlook. When we change our attitude about our trials, they will change our lives for good!

It is important for us to understand that joy is not the same thing as pleasure. God has never called us to enjoy our difficulties! Yet He has challenged us to "...rejoice in our sufferings, because we know that suffering produces perseverance; perseverance, character; and character, hope. And hope does not disappoint us, because God has poured out his love into our hearts by the Holy Spirit, whom he has given us" (Romans 5:3-5; New International Version).

As Christians, we can experience joy in all kinds of unpleasurable circumstances when we comprehend the fact that persevering faith will eventually pay off! The results will always be increased maturity and fruitfulness. Although it is natural for us to want to get rid of our problems, God is interested in the development of our character. He is concerned primarily with how we respond to the pressures of life, and he understands better than anyone else that we can only grow in tough times.

Calvin Miller, a Christian author, illustrated this truth beautifully when he wrote,

> Scottish patriarchs looking for walking sticks, always passed over the untried wood of the lower slopes, climbing to the weathered heights to search for rods made strong by storm and wind. For these young trees once fought the icy Northers and with each fight they bent and twisted and broke a bit inside. But gradually each inner scar became the steely fiber, brought by every storm that they endured.
>
> These are the Rods of God!
>
> Ask Moses!
>
> Such Rods can speak to a threatened Pharaoh, or order Suez water-walls to let the children pass. Such rods will make a cobra. Lightning rises off their knobby heads.
>
> But do not let their majesty delude you! These mighty rods were once just spindly trees. Bless not the rod, but rather bless the gales that broke their sinews, lacing them with stone, 'till the storms they so despised had changed them into scepters: such maces make Midianites and shepherds to be Kings.
>
> So all real saints are fashioned in the crucible of God. They are broken—even crushed—between mortar and pestle; then their soft nothingness is changed to granite, from which God fashions monuments to himself. Thus, a Jew of Tarsus was beaten, stoned, shipwrecked, imprisoned (2 Cor. 11:23ff),

and yet he speaks out in praise, of the brokenness that forged him! Paul does not brag of being strong! He boasts only of his weakness and praises the storms (2 Cor. 12:10). For in his heart he knew that simple grace has little volume in its soft authority. But when such grace is battered by the storms, the gales do their transforming work. Thus grace and brokenness together can take a frightened Asian Jew and name him Thunder, the Lion of God.[1]

How are we holding up under the pressures of the moment? Are they making us bitter or better? Are they driving us further from God or closer to Him? Are they producing an attitude of despondency or a spirit of brokenness?

In Jeremiah 18:1-6, we are introduced to one of the many "job descriptions" of our heavenly Father. It is here in this passage that He is simply referred to as " the potter." It was at the potter's house that the marred vessel was broken and made into another vessel.

The Potter's ability to shape human lives is a recurring theme throughout Scripture. The Holy Spirit wants to use this very word picture of the potter at the potter's wheel to capture our imaginations. We watch as the Master Artist carefully forms and shapes the mass of clay. As His skilled hands apply pressure and the clay becomes pliable and yields to the Potter's touch, a usable vessel begins to take shape.

Although the Potter creates and forms with hands of pressure, it is always sensitive, loving, "positive" pressure. He knows as He works the clay just how much stress it can take. The same Hands that apply the pressure also protect the emerging vessel.

When individuals fly the "friendly skies" of commercial airlines, pressure is absolutely necessary. Without a "pressurized" atmosphere, the cabin of the airplane would literally become a deathtrap for the passengers. The "positive" pressure they experience during flight is designed to maintain and promote life. This "pressurized" environment enables the passengers to soar at altitudes not normally possible!

The pressure of the Potter's hands upon our lives must never be viewed as something negative. Our Father always fashions us with divine wisdom! He continúes to work on us to encourage us to yield to His touch. He keeps calling forth from the clay of our lives the response He desires. His "pressurized" touch is vital if we, as earthen vessels, are going to be filled with Living Water that is to be poured out on behalf of others!

OUR PATTERN FOR BROKENNESS

Undoubtedly, the greatest example of brokenness is Jesus Himself! Brokenness was the lens through which He viewed all of His surroundings. It affected His perception, as well as His attitudes, toward everything. If we are going to emulate our Saviour, we need to think as He thought and to see things through His eyes.

In Philippians 2:5-8, Paul challenged us about this very issue: "Have this attitude in yourselves which was also in Christ Jesus, who, although He existed in the form of God, did not regard equality with God a thing to be grasped, but emptied himself, taking the form of a bondservant, and being made in the likeness of men. And being found in appearance as a man, He humbled himself by becoming obedient to the point of death, even death on a cross" (New American Standard Version).

What did Paul mean when he admonished us to have the same attitude as that of Christ? The key to the answer is found in verse seven, where we are told that Jesus "emptied himself." In theological terms, this is referred to as Christ's kenosis or "self-emptying" and is derived from the Greek term which occurs in this verse.

Of what did Christ empty Himself? According to the seventh and eighth verses, it is clear that Jesus emptied Himself of His divine privileges. This does not mean that Jesus gave up His divinity; instead, it means that He voluntarily gave up the freedom, glory and honor that was due Him as God. In other words, He gave up the right to be Himself when He became a man.

Most of us resist the idea of giving up the right to be ourselves. Instead we often promote the "right" as a necessary requirement for finding fulfillment. Yet, the Bible clearly instructs us that we will not really find ourselves until we lose ourselves in God. All too often we try to justify our selfish behavior with such excuses as, "I'm just like my father" or "I'm an only child" or "I'm a middle child" or "I came from an abusive home." While we should never deny or ignore real hurts that need healing, we need to get beyond the popular idea of acting out who we think we are. This attitude encourages us to put our own interests before the interests of others.

In contrast, the attitude of brokenness always compels us to put the interests of others before our own. This is not co-dependency. This is healthy! Some of the most neurotic people are those who are stuck on themselves. In his book, *MEN AND WOMEN*, Larry Crabb, a Christian author, wrote, "All our relationship problems spring from one place—the foul well of selfishness. More than anything, what gets in the way of getting along is self-centeredness that seems reasonable [my right]. Poor communication, temper problems, unhealthy responses to dysfunctional family backgrounds, co-dependent relationships, and personal incompatibility—everything (unless medically caused) flows out of the cesspool of self-centeredness."[2]

The kenosis or self-emptying process requires giving up our lives, interests and rights and embracing the cross. It is the crucifixion of the "self-life." When Jesus emptied Himself, He was then able to fulfill the role of a servant [slave]. He not only gave up the right to be who He really was, He even gave up the right to be something! If anyone had the right to make something of His life, it was the Son of God. Yet He willingly chose to serve dying humanity, and "...give His life a ransom for many" (Matthew 20:28). Jesus did make something of His life, but He did it the broken way, through servanthood!

As human beings, we spend a great deal of energy trying to make something of ourselves. We are constantly surrounded by messages that drive us to be self-motivated. "You only go around once in life!" "Just do it!" "Be all that you can be!" Because we are always encouraged to seek self-expression and self-recognition, the way of brokenness presents a real crisis in our lives. The reason for this is not difficult to understand, for a servant or slave has nothing, is nothing and never expects to be anything. Furthermore, the world does not know or care if he exists. Only by taking on the mind of Christ can we ever submit to such a life of servanthood.

God is calling each of us to face the crisis of kenosis. Without the emptying of self with its goals and interests, there can be no reproduction of the divine image. Jesus is our pattern; what happened to him must happen to us. If it does not, then the pathway into the resurrection power of Christ will be closed to us.

God never calls anyone to a life of mediocrity; He expects us to be spiritually motivated in all that we do. However, the attitude of brokenness is always essential for the purifying of our ambitions! What motivates us? What are our ambitions? If, for example, we have come to like the power and influence of a particular ministry the Lord has given us, we need to disown it by giving it back to Him. If we get so involved in our careers, families or possessions that we do not have time for the Lord, we need to be reminded again of the attitude of brokenness.

We are extremely vulnerable when our fulfillment comes from sources other than our relationship with God. We need to lay each source on the altar; we need to recommit them to Him, recognizing that they are all God's, not ours.

The disciple of Jesus recognizes that all things are owned by the Father and we are merely His stewards. He has entrusted us with gifts, talents, resources and relationships which we are responsible for managing and developing. We will never be able to follow in Christ's footsteps as true servants until we quit thinking we are owners and stop trying to make something of ourselves with the gifts, talents, resources and relationships that have only been loaned to us.

As a broken Savior, Jesus also gave up the right to be respected. Philippians 2:8 tells us "...He humbled Himself and became obedient to the point of death, even the death of the cross." What a death it was! Jesus was crucified between two thieves. The association with these two criminals left no doubt as to what His accusers thought of Him. This was death in its worst form! Crucifixion was a slow and excruciating execution used by Rome to deter crime. People were brought face to face with all the gore of the moment. They would come and mock those being punished, venting their anger on the ones who had committed crimes against society.

Jesus easily could have destroyed His enemies. He could have called 10,000 angels to rescue Him from impending death. Yet Jesus was not threatened by the attempts of His accusers to make Him nothing. He had given up His right to be who He really was; He had given up the right to be respected. The restraint required for the Creator of the universe to allow His creation to purposefully end His life is beyond imagination. His brokenness, however, constituted the mightiest power the world has ever known!

Do we want personal revival at such a price? If we are going to experience the resurrection life and power of Christ in a way we have never known before, we must hold nothing back from our Father. He who gave everything demands everything from us! Even the dearest things to our hearts, including our reputations, must be brought to the Cross.

There was a time in the life of Charles Haddon Spurgeon when he was subjected to slander and criticism because of his passion for Jesus and his desire to take the Gospel to the people. This powerful English preacher said in an 1857 sermon, "I shall never forget the circumstance when, after I thought I had made a full consecration to Christ, a slanderous report against my character came to my ears, and my heart was broken in agony because I should have to lose that, in preaching Christ's Gospel. I fell on my knees, and said, 'Master, I will not keep back even my character from Thee. If I must lose that too, then let it go; it is the dearest thing I have; but it shall go, if, like my Master, they shall say that I have a devil, and am mad.'"[3]

The entire sacrifice of our lives must be laid on the altar to be consumed by the fire from Heaven. This is why death is so often associated with seasons of brokenness. The smell of death is always in the air during the breaking process. Jesus' obedience led to His death! If we are truly going to follow Christ, our destination must ultimately be the cross (Matthew 16:24).

It is certainly much easier to "confess" Christ than it is to follow Him. The thought of death troubles us. We want to manage our lives because we do not know where Jesus will lead us or what He will require of us. Yet we are never really safe until we have taken our hands off the controls of our lives and given up the right to ourselves. John Calvin's motto must become ours: "I give Thee all: I keep back nothing for myself."[4]

Feeling a sense of loss is perfectly normal during the breaking process because a part of us is being put to death. Our emotional responses during times of brokenness often have similarities to the grieving process. Initially we may feel a sense of shock and numbness. This can lead to a stage of denial, when we have difficulty dealing with what has just taken place. A period of extreme pain and confusion usually follows as we grope for answers to the haunting questions that flood our minds. Feelings of hopelessness and despair often come next. We may even find ourselves struggling with anger as we try to understand why God allowed the circumstances in the first place. This is all a part of the breaking process as we mourn our own death, the death of "self."

There is a time to weep! It is a gut-wrenching feeling! Yet Jesus said, "Blessed are those who mourn, For they shall be comforted" (Matthew 5:4). The word "blessed" means happy or contented. What a paradox—happy are the sad! How can this be? How can we be happy and content as we find ourselves losing the grip on our lives? Our Father has given us the assurance through His promise that He will make everything beautiful in its time (Ecclesiates 3:11). If we will allow Him to heal our wounds as He walks us through the various stages of grieving, joy will come in the morning!

Years ago, there was a minister who had a congregation that continually refused to accept his message. He wanted to lead his people into a knowledge of Christ, but they were unwilling to follow. Whenever he stood up to preach, he felt as if Satan were standing next to him, resisting him. Things became so bad that he even had to ask the choir to resign. The choir not only resigned but also persuaded the rest of the congregation to stop singing. From that point on, the only singing was done by the preacher.

One day, as he found himself at his wits' end, the Lord spoke to him through an odd set of circumstances. He was sitting in a park when he saw part of a newspaper lying on the ground. As he looked at the torn piece of paper, his eyes fell upon these words: "No man is ever fully accepted until he has, first of all, been utterly rejected." For him, this was all that needed to be said. He had been completely rejected by man, yet the recognition of the fact that he was fully accepted by God began a period of fruitful ministry in another area that lasted for years.

When we trust our heavenly Father, we do not need to defend ourselves. Being broken means letting Him take over our public relations department. "For to this you were called, because Christ also suffered for us, leaving us an example, that you should follow His steps: 'Who committed no sin, Nor was deceit found in His mouth'; who, when He was reviled, did not revile in return; when He suffered, He did not threaten, but committed Himself to Him who judges righteously" (1 Peter 2:21-23).

We are told in Philippians 2:9-11 that because Jesus emptied Himself and became obedient to death "...God also has highly exalted Him and given Him the name which is above every name, that at the name of Jesus every knee should bow, of those in heaven, and of those on earth, and of those under the earth, and that every tongue should confess that Jesus Christ is Lord, to the glory of God the Father." The One who willingly became the least has become the greatest!

If we are willing to take on the attitude of Christ, He will advance us in His time and in His way. The way to promotion in the Kingdom of God does not come by seeing how much we can obtain or how big we can get or how far we can go. Rather, promotion comes as we are willing to embrace the mind of Christ. The building of the kind of ministry that can impart life to others only comes when our lives are enlarged by brokenness.

Margaret Clarkson summed it up best with these words: "Perhaps the greatest good that suffering can work for a believer is to increase the capacity of his soul for God. The greater our need, the greater will be our capacity; the greater our capacity, the greater will be our experience of God. Can any price be too much for such eternal good?"[5]

BROKEN VASES

The aroma of extravagant love.
So pure. So lovely.
Flowing from the veined alabaster vase
of Mary's broken heart—
A heart broken against the hard reality
of her Savior's imminent death.
Mingled with tears, the perfume became—
by some mysterious chemistry of Heaven—
Not diluted but more concentrated,
Potent enough behind the ears of each century
for the scent to linger to this day.
Doubtless, the fragrance, absorbed by his garment,
as it flowed from his head,
Accompanied Christ through the humiliation of his trials,
the indignity of his mockings,
the pain of his beatings,
the inhumanity of his cross.
Through the heavy smell of sweat and blood,
A hint of that fragrance must have arisen
from his garment—
Until, at shameful last, the garment was stripped
and gambled away.
And maybe, just maybe, it was that scent
amid the stench of humanity rabbled around the cross,
that gave the Savior the strength to say:
"Father, forgive them, for they know not what they do."

And as Mary walked away from the cross,
The same scent probably still lingered in the now-limp hair
she used to dry the Savior's feet—
A reminder of the love that spilled
from his broken alabaster body.
So pure. So lovely.
So truly extravagant.
It was a vase he never regretted breaking.
Nor did she.

Ken Gire

Chapter Seven

COOPERATING WITH CONVICTION

The late Dr. Samuel Chadwick of Cliff College, England, once told the story of a special conference weekend that was held on the school campus. The college grounds were crowded with visitors. All the facilities for accommodating and feeding the guests were utilized to their capacity. At the height of the convention, for some unknown reason, the water supply failed. The faucets could only produce a small trickle. Plumbers were quickly called in to investigate the problem. After some time, they located the section of pipe-line which seemed to be the source of the malfunction. As they searched further, they discovered that the pipe had cracked and a fat toad had squeezed in and squatted crosswise, virtually cutting off the water supply.

Sin is the toad that squats across the life-line of our lives and restricts the outflow of divine life and power. In his book, *BY MY SPIRIT*, Jonathan Goforth wrote that "...all hindrance in the Church is due to sin....It is sin in individual Church members, whether at home or on the foreign field, which grieves and quenches the Holy Spirit."

It was out of deep personal conviction that Mr. Goforth wrote these words. While working as a missionary in China in 1905, he was given a little pamphlet containing selections from *THE AUTOBIOGRAPHY OF CHARLES FINNEY* and *LECTURES ON REVIVAL*. On the front page there was a sentence that clearly stated that it was useless for Christians to expect revival by simply asking for it without bothering to fulfill the laws which determine spiritual blessing. As soon as Goforth read the statement, he said, "If Finney is right, then I'm going to find out what those laws are and obey them, no matter what it costs."

He later wrote,

> In the autumn of 1906, having felt depressed for some time by the cold and fruitless condition of my out-stations, I was preparing to set out on a tour to see what could be done to revive them. There was a matter, however, between the Lord and myself, that had to be straightened out before He could use me. I need not go into the details. Suffice to say that there was a difference between a brother missionary and myself. I honestly felt that I was in the right. (Such, of course, is very human. In any difference it is always safe to divide by half). At any rate, the pressure from the Spirit was quite plain. It was that I should go and make that thing straight. I kept answering back to God that the fault was the other man's, not mine; that it was up to him to come to me, not for me to go to him.

> The pressure continued. 'But Lord,' I expostulated, 'he came to my study and in tears confessed his fault. So, isn't the thing settled?' 'You hypocrite!' I seemed to hear Him say, 'you know that you are not loving each other as brethren, as I commanded you to.' Still I held out. The fault was the other man's, I kept insisting; surely, therefore, I couldn't be expected to do anything about it. Then came the final word, 'If you don't straighten this thing out before you go on that trip, you must expect to fail. I can't go with you.' That humbled me somewhat. I did not

feel at all easy about going on that long and difficult tour without His help. Well I knew that by myself I would be like one beating the air.

The night before I was to start out on my trip I had to lead the prayer-meeting for the Chinese Christians. All the way out to the church the pressure continued: 'Go and straighten this thing out, so that I may go with you tomorrow.' Still I wouldn't yield. I started the meeting. It was all right while they were singing a hymn and during the reading of Scripture. But as soon as I opened my lips in prayer I became confused, for all the time the Spirit kept saying: 'You hypocrite! Why don't you straighten this thing out?' I became still more troubled while delivering the short prayer-address. Finally, when about half-way through my talk the burden became utterly intolerable, I yielded. 'Lord,' I promised in my heart, 'as soon as this meeting is over, I'll go and make that matter right.' Instantly something in the audience seemed to snap. My Chinese hearers couldn't tell what was going on in my heart; yet in a moment the whole atmosphere was changed. Upon the meeting being thrown open for prayer, one after another rose to their feet to pray, only to break down weeping. For almost twenty years we missionaries had been working among the Honanese, and had longed in vain to see a tear of penitence roll down a Chinese cheek.

It was late that night when the meeting closed. As soon as I could get away I hastened over to the house of my brother missionary, only to find that the lights were out and that the whole family were in bed. Not wishing to disturb them I went back to my home. But the difficulty was settled. Next morning, before daybreak, I was on my way to the first out-station. The results of that tour far exceeded anything that I had dared hope for. At each place the spirit of judgment was made manifest. Wrongs were righted and crooked things were made straight. At one place I was only able to spend a single night, but that night all present broke down. In the following year one out-station more than doubled its numbers; to another fifty-four members were added, and to another eighty-eight.[1]

This all happened because one man was eventually willing to yield to the convicting work of the Holy Spirit in his life! Likewise, if the purposes of God are to be experienced in our lives, as well as in our generation, it is essential that we also learn how to cooperate with the convictions of the Spirit. From the very first step of salvation to the fullness of what God has for us in Christ, His dealings with us always begin with conviction! It is impossible for God to work in our lives unless we welcome this process and respond to it properly.

What, then, is the nature of true conviction, and how do we willingly embrace it in our lives? Conviction is being "searched out" by the Holy Spirit; it is being made conscious of sin by the Spirit's work in our hearts.

Conviction is not self-analysis! The prophet Jeremiah wrote, "The heart is deceitful above all things, And desperately wicked; Who can know it? I, the Lord, search the heart..." (Jeremiah 17:9-10). None of us truly knows or understands his own heart. We are far too easily deceived in not recognizing our own personal sins! Only the Holy Spirit can probe deep within the recesses of our hearts and bring to the surface those things that keep us from loving Him more fully.

Scripture clearly reveals that one of the primary works of the Holy Spirit on behalf of man, whether saved or unsaved, is the work of conviction. In John 16:8 we read, "And when He [the Holy Spirit] has come, He will convict the world of sin, and of righteousness, and of judgment." Conviction is seen as one of the main activities of the Holy Spirit because man's first need is a knowledge of sin. It is an eye-opening fact that man is really unconscious of sin until he is made aware of it by the Spirit of God.

In his booklet entitled, *CONTINUOUS REVIVAL*, Norman Grubb wrote that "...Sin is a revelation. It is God who graciously shows us sin, even as it is He who shows us the precious blood. Sin is only seen to be SIN—against God—when He reveals it; otherwise sin may just be known as a wrong against a brother, or an anti-social act, or an inconvenience, or a disability, or some such thing. Indeed that is often the extent of the message of a 'social gospel,' to be rid of sin as a hindrance to brotherhood, as an inconvenience to human progress; not as coming short of the glory of God. God shows us sin."[2]

It is vital that we respond properly to the Holy Spirit when He begins dealing with us about specific issues in our lives. God has never called us to continually look inside ourselves. He does not require of us lives of introspection or unhealthy self-examination but, instead, lives of absolute honesty and cooperation with His Spirit.

Therefore, the first thing true conviction should work in us is honest confession of our sin. True confession is an acceptance of God's own assessment of our sin, accompanied by a godly sorrow that produces repentance. We must see what God sees in order to be truly repentant. Honest confession recognizes the sin that God seeks to put His finger on in our lives and naming it just as He names it. The Greek word "confess" literally means "to agree with" or "to speak the same language." We must say what God says about our sins and call them by their rightful names.

For example, when the Spirit of God graciously confronts the pride in our lives, He expects us to name it as such, for pride is more hideous in the sight of God than what we might call a "lack of humility." The reason some of us are never liberated from certain persistent sins is because the work of conviction is not able to go to the heart of the problem. We continually let ourselves off the hook by skirting the real issue and confessing to a lack of some virtue rather than calling the sin by its true name. It is a lot easier on the ego to ask for forgiveness for a "lack of humility" than to confess the sin of pride.

How many individuals are still struggling with personal issues, such as anger, because it is far more convenient to admit to a "lack of love" than it is to call the thing what it really is—the sin of hatred and animosity (1 John 3:15)? We human beings have always been prone to rationalization. From the first moment Adam sinned in the Garden, man has sought to escape from the voice of God. Like Adam, we still find ourselves struggling with the tendency to cover our sin and hide behind various excuses. Man is so inclined whenever the voice of the Spirit comes to the heart in the form of conviction.

This tendency causes us to blame our circumstances instead of dealing with our own personal and moral failures. It certainly is more comfortable to talk about our "bad nerves" than it is to confess our "irritability" as sin. How many of us would rather blame the "other guy" than admit to the sin of bitterness and rejection? And who wants to repent of the sin of self-pity?

Several years ago, an article was written in the *BASICALLY BUSINESS NEWSLETTER* entitled, "The Lighter Side of Kamikaze Pedestrians and Such" and reads as follows:

> Accidents will happen. When they do, though, it's usually 'the other guy's fault.' Here are some telling remarks taken from actual insurance claim files:

"The other car collided with mine without giving warning of its intentions."

"An invisible car came out of nowhere, struck my vehicle and vanished."

" I'd been driving for forty years, when I fell asleep at the wheel and had an accident."

"A pedestrian hit me and went under my car."

"Coming home, I drove into the wrong house and collided with a tree I don't have."

"As I approached the intersection, a sign suddenly appeared in a place where no sign had ever been before. So I was unable to stop in time to avoid an accident."

"The pedestrian had no idea which direction to run, so I ran over him."

"The telephone pole was approaching. I was attempting to swerve out of the way when it struck my front end."

"I pulled away from the side of the road, glanced at my mother-in-law and headed over the embankment."

"As I reached the intersection, a hedge sprang up obscuring my vision. I just didn't see the other car."

"The guy was all over the road, and I had to swerve a number of times before hitting him."

"My car was legally parked when it backed into the other vehicle."[3]

Obviously, some of these excuses were simply the result of miscommunication. Yet they all reveal the human tendency toward rationalization. If nothing else, these explanations certainly have a familiar ring to them. How many times have we justified our attitudes and actions by suggesting, "I've always been like that" or "I can't help it...I'm just human" or "Oh, that's just me"? Such excuses, however, not only take the "sting" out of sin and disobedience, they also encourage us to treat lightly or completely ignore the Spirit's work of conviction in our lives.

The word "excuse" has been defined as the skin of the reason stuffed with lies. This definition, although humorous, is absolutely true. What are excuses, anyway, in the light of eternity? Any time we feel the urge to defend or justify our sins, we need to stop long enough to ask the following questions: "Will this excuse be accepted by God when I stand before Him one day?" "Would I be willing to justify this sin if I knew it would keep me out of heaven?"

If Satan can get us to excuse our attitudes and actions by renaming what God calls sin, he has succeeded in deceiving us. In turn, the precious convictions of God become unproductive in our lives because the Holy Spirit deals in truth and truth alone. Pseudo-confessions make it impossible for God to effectively deal with us; consequently, many people fail to experience the power of grace to overcome sin. Grace only comes to the truly repentant heart.

A.W. Tozer wrote,

> ...I've heard for the last thirty years that repentance is a change of mind, and I believe it, of course, as far as it goes. But that's just what's the matter with us. We have reduced repentance to a change of mind. It is a mental act, indeed, but I point out that repentance is not likely to do us much good until it ceases to be a change of mind only and becomes a

wound within our spirit. No man has truly repented until his sin has wounded him near to death, until the wound has broken him and defeated him and taken all the fight and self-assurance out of him and he sees himself as the one who nailed his Saviour on the tree.

I don't know about you, but the only way I can keep right with God is to keep contrite, to keep a sense of contrition upon my spirit. Now there's a lot of cheap and easy getting rid of sin and getting your repentance disposed of. But the great Christians, in and out of the Bible, have been those who were wounded with a sense of contrition so that they never quite got over the thought and the feeling that they personally had crucified Jesus. The great Bishop Ussher each week used to go down by the riverbank and there all Saturday afternoon kneel by a log and bewail his sins before his God. Perhaps that was the secret of his greatness.[4]

True conviction will always work in us a godly sorrow for sin. However, the Spirit's purpose in convicting us is not to condemn us; instead, He seeks to not only forgive us of our sin but also uproot from our hearts the specific sin of which He has convicted us. Spiritual surgery is always painful! In the words of W. Graham Scroggie: "There has never been a revival which did not begin with an acute [cutting, penetrating] sense of sin."[5] It is really immaterial whether we are talking about personal revival or corporate revival within the Church as a whole. Conviction of sin accompanied by true repentance is an indispensable part of revival.

During the Welsh Revival (1904-1905) in which more than 100,000 people were converted in the space of five months, Evan Roberts repeatedly hammered away at the issues of repentance and confession of sin. His four points were:

1. The past must be made clear by confession of every known sin to God and every known wrong done to man.

2. Every doubtful thing in the believer's life must be put away.

3. Prompt and implicit obedience must be rendered to the Spirit of God.

4. Public confession of Christ must be made within and with out the church.

Reporting on this revival, Dr. G. Campbell Morgan observed that the outpouring of the Spirit was characterized by "...the most remarkable confessions of sin—confessions that were costly."[6] In fact, he heard people who had been church members and even church officers stand and confess hidden sin in their hearts, impurities committed and overlooked, and then ask for the prayers of their Christian friends for cleansing and forgiveness.

Without genuine repentance there can be no revival, personal or corporate. How could it be any different? If through the precious gift of repentance we are ushered into the Kingdom of God, how can we, as Christians, ever expect to walk in continuous revival apart from living in an attitude of repentance?

Nothing is more basic to the life of a believer than repentance—nothing more liberating or life-giving! Repentance is a key foundation of the Christian life because it is the only proper attitude we can have toward a holy God. This is why Satan has tried to tarnish the message of repentance as much as he has by causing some believers to immediately think of condemnation and intimidation. Yet nothing could be further from the truth. The Bible speaks of "...repentance leading to salvation" (2 Corinthians 7:10) and "...repentance to life" (Acts 11:18). There is nothing condemning about that! Instead, repentance is a wonderful gift of God's grace.

Repentance is always seen in Scripture as a gift. It is God who grants repentance, just as He gives faith to believe. None of us can bring ourselves to repentance. No one is capable of changing his heart from being hardened by sin to weeping over sin. Only God can change the condition of the human heart. However, when we acknowledge our need, the Holy Spirit's influence in our lives enables us to turn from our sin.

This turning from sin is really the true meaning of repentance. The Old Testament word for repent means "to turn"—to walk in one direction and then turn and walk in the opposite direction. It speaks of turning from sin and moving toward God. In the New Testament, the term "repent" means "to change or turn the mind." It applies to changing our minds about sin to the point of turning away from it.

There are occasions in Scripture when a form of the word "repent" is translated "to feel regret." Although an individual should feel regret for his sin when he repents, merely feeling regret is not the same as experiencing genuine repentance. Judas, for example, bitterly regretted betraying Jesus. Although he was remorseful for what he had done, he did not change. Instead, he went out and committed suicide.

True repentance is not just remorse. Many people regret what they have done, not because of how they have grieved the Lord but because of the serious consequences of their sin. Oswald Chambers said, "Never mistake remorse for repentance; remorse simply puts a man in hell while he is on earth, it carries no remedial quality with it at all, nothing that betters a man...Repentance is not a reaction, remorse is. Remorse is—I will never do the thing again [but it is only a temporary emotion without any power to change]. Repentance is that I deliberately become the opposite to what I have been...The disposition of the Son of God can only enter my life by the road to repentance."[7]

The truly repentant individual not only recognizes that he is guilty before God but also acknowledges it. He understands that his sin has personally offended the Lord and grieved the precious Holy Spirit. The repentant person willingly gives up his resistance to and rebellion against God and His Word. He embraces God's rule in his life. He changes his mind toward everything and, accordingly, changes his ways so that he no longer continues in sin.

The truly repentant individual is uncompromising with personal sin. He understands that its pleasures are deceptive and will pollute and poison his life. He sees beyond the present moment and refuses to cast aside the reality of death and judgment. He recognizes that his sin will ultimately destroy him and damn him eternally. He cannot continue to live in it any longer. He must be free at any price!

Some of us, however, still find ourselves bound by certain sins, and nothing we do seems to break our chains. This bondage is often caused by shallow repentance. We want to be forgiven, but we do not want to completely turn from our sin. We want to be free from the consequences of our sin, but we hold out the possibility of committing the same sin again because it still holds an **attraction** for us. We have not truly disowned the sin that has now captured our hearts.

We must also admit that it is not always easy to break free from particular sins, especially if we have been caught in their ugly web. Yet if we will sincerely cry out to God for freedom, then the Lord will give us the grace to repent and the power to overcome. Genuine repentance produces deep, lasting change. We will not only be ashamed of our sin but hate it and turn away from it!

True repentance will also result in works of righteousness in the believer's life. In Matthew 3:8, John the Baptist said to the religious leaders who came to his baptism, "Do those things that prove you have turned to God and have changed the way you think and act."

(God's Word translation). Several decades ago, there was a spiritual awakening in South Africa. The police authorities were amazed at the genuine repentance and restitution made not only by converts but by backsliders who had been restored to the Lord. The *DAILY DISPATCH* of East London, South Africa, listed the following articles returned by repentant believers: "80 sheets, 25 blankets, 24 jackets, 34 trousers, 11 overcoats, 6 women's coats, 25 dresses, 27 skirts, 50 shirts, 22 bedspreads, 64 hats, 23 towels, 1 table, 4 chairs, 50 pillow slips, 15 scissors, 5 hairclippers, 9 wallets, 4 cameras, 4 wrist watches, 3 revolvers and ammunition, 30 tumblers and an assortment of jewelry, tools, cigarette lighters, crockery, cutlery, boots and shoes, pressure stoves, frying pans, lanterns, and safety razors."[8]

During an outpouring of the Spirit in the city of Belfast, Ireland, under the ministry of W. P. Nicholson, there was such a spirit of repentance and restitution in evidence that workers at a well-known shipyard returned enough material to the authorities to build and equip a sizable machine shed. These are the life-giving effects of true repentance! Repentance not only produces a change of heart but also a change of conduct.

How can we develop and maintain a lifestyle of repentance? First, we need to continually ask ourselves some tough questions: "Am I playing around with a particular sin, trying to get as close to the fire as I can without getting burned?" "Am I engaging in superficial repentance, making excuses to people and to God instead of confessing my sin?" "Am I trying to convince myself that there is a measurable difference between big sins and little sins, even though the most prevalent sins among believers—criticism and fault-finding—are contemptible sins in God's eyes (Proverbs 6:16-19)?" "Am I more concerned about my reputation before people than my character before the Lord?"

We also need to agree quickly with the Holy Spirit's evaluation of our spiritual condition. A truly repentant heart says, "Father, I am guilty of sinning against you. I deserve punishment, but I humbly ask you to be merciful to me and forgive me. Give me the grace to obey so that I will not continue to sin." By being absolutely honest, we will keep from grieving and resisting the Lord.

At this point, however, we need to differentiate between the conviction of the Holy Spirit and the condemnation of the Devil. Satan's accusations are very general, leaving us with a sense of hopelessness and a cloud of depression. The Holy Spirit, on the other hand, always convicts us of specific issues. He not only shows us our need but also gives us hope for the future and encouragement to press on. The Father's arms are always open to the one whose heart is truly repentant before Him (Luke 15:11-32).

After we have repented, we need to actually believe we have been forgiven. We easily find ourselves falling prey to false guilt and shame for days and even weeks. It is one thing to feel genuine sorrow for our sins; it is another thing to continually brow-beat ourselves with condemnation.

In all honesty, however, our self-inflicted shame is often the result of disguised pride. Under the pretense of humility, we are actually claiming that our sin is too big and too much for Christ to forgive. Pride refuses to embrace total forgiveness. True humility, on the other hand, freely accepts mercy.

Finally, to live in a continual attitude of repentance, we need to learn to keep short accounts with the Holy Spirit. We must be willing to humble ourselves and deal with sin immediately, being open to the convictions of the Spirit at all times and willing to "break" when God puts His finger on anything throughout the day. This attitude will not only create within us a heightened sensitivity toward sin but will also keep our consciences clean and our spirits free. Eugenie de Guerin wrote, "When the soul has laid down its faults at the feet of God, it feels as though it had wings." It is time we soar on the winds of the Spirit! It is time to be free![9]

LORD, EMANCIPATE

These doubts and fears,
For many years,
Have fettered up my soul.
O blessed Lord,
Emancipate;
Come now and take control.

I now aspire
With strong desire
To be a channel clean.
O blessed Lord,
Emancipate;
Reign o'er my life supreme.

Oh, take me higher,
Endue with fire,
Thy glory dwell within!
O blessed Lord,
Emancipate
And keep me free from sin!

Now free from sin,
Endue within;
Give Thy compassion—tears.
Thou dost, my Lord,
Emancipate;
Restore my wasted years.

At any loss
I choose Thy cross.
Earth's values I deplore.
Thy blood doth now
Emancipate;
Thy victory I adore

Leonard Ravenhill

Chapter Eight

SONS OF FRESH OIL (ONE)

Although the word "anointing" is used extensively today in Christian circles, very few believers understand the significance of the term. The word "anoint" literally means "to rub" and carries with it the idea of "smearing with oil." The concept of the anointing goes back thousands of years and meant in its simplest form to set apart or consecrate something or someone to a special task by the pouring on of oil.

Jacob, for example, in fleeing from the anger of his brother Esau, made his way to a place called Haran. As night fell, he lay down to sleep with a rock for a pillow (Genesis 28:11). He dreamed of a ladder that reached to heaven with angels ascending and descending upon it. When Jacob awoke in the morning, "...he was afraid and said, 'How awesome is this place! This is none other than the house of God, and this is the gate of heaven!' Then Jacob rose early in the morning, and took the stone that he had put at his head, set it up as a pillar, and poured oil on top of it" (vs.17-18). Later, God spoke to Jacob and said, "I am the God of Bethel, where you **anointed** the pillar " (Genesis 31:13).*

When God gave specific details for the ordaining of the priesthood under the Old Covenant, He instructed Moses that Aaron and his sons had to be **anointed** in order to minister to Him as priests (Exodus 28:41).* It was because of the anointing that Aaron and his sons were consecrated and set apart for the service of the Lord.

115

When God sent the prophet Samuel to select another king to replace Saul, and David was chosen, the Lord said to Samuel, "...'Arise, **anoint** him; for this is the one!' Then Samuel took the horn of oil and anointed him in the midst of his brothers; and the Spirit of the Lord came upon David from that day forward...." (1 Samuel 16:12-13).*

When Elijah fled from Jezebel and later met with God at Horeb, the Lord instructed him to **anoint** three individuals. Jehu was to be anointed as king of Israel; Hazael was to be the king over Syria; and Elisha was to be anointed as the prophet who would take Elijah's place (1 Kings 19:15-16).

Throughout the Old Testament, prophets, priests and kings were anointed and set apart for special duties. Interestingly enough, at the age of thirty Jesus was also **anointed** for His Father's service as Prophet, Priest and King. However, in the case of Jesus, John 3:34 tells us that the Holy Spirit came mightily upon Him "...without measure or limit" (New Living Translation).

Under the New Covenant we believers have also been consecrated and set apart for a special task. 1 Peter 2:9 informs the Christian that "...you are a chosen people. You are a kingdom of priests, God's holy nation, his very own possession. This is so you can show others the goodness of God" (New Living Translation). This truth is further reinforced in Revelation 5:9-10 where we read, "And they sang a new song, saying: 'You are worthy to take the scroll, And to open its seals; For You were slain, And have redeemed us to God by Your blood Out of every tribe and tongue and people and nation, And have made us kings and priests to our God; And we shall reign on the earth.'"

As kings and priests of the New Covenant, each of us has been anointed and set apart by the Holy Spirit for the service of the Lord (1 John 2:20,27). We are members of the Body of Christ; Jesus is the "Anointed One." Those of us who make up His Body have received His anointing because He lives in us by His Spirit. However, to experience the full release of the Spirit in our lives, we must first understand the true nature of "the anointing" and what is required of us.

All too often we equate the anointing with certain spiritual gifts (1 Corinthians 12:8-10), not realizing that the degree of anointing in an individual is directly related to his submission to the Holy Spirit in the personal development of godly character. Many people have been given wonderful gifts, but because the fruit of the Spirit (Galatians 5:22-23) has not been adequately developed in them, their lives remain ineffective. The Spirit's maturing of Christ-like character in each of us serves to enhance the gifts and bring them forth with grace and mercy. The nature of the anointing requires that we have an understanding of the process whereby it is actively released in our lives.

INGREDIENTS OF THE HOLY ANOINTING OIL

Although the anointing oil of Old Testament times was essentially a perfume, its ingredients hold tremendous significance for us today; they were divinely chosen to illustrate the various ways in which God prepares an individual for an anointed life and ministry.

Throughout history God has often used symbolism to speak to His people. When God gave Moses instructions for the preparing of the anointing oil, He said, "Collect choice spices—12½ pounds of pure myrrh, 6¼ pounds each of cinnamon and of sweet cane, 12½ pounds of cassia, and one gallon of olive oil. Blend these ingredients into a holy anointing oil" (Exodus 30:23-25, New Living Translation).

117

PURE MYRRH

Myrrh was a fragrant resin that oozed from a tiny shrub. Although it was bitter to the taste, it produced such a pleasant fragrance that it had great value in biblical times. The word "myrrh" literally means "bitter." It was one of the three gifts brought to Jesus at His birth. The gift of gold depicted His deity; the gift of frankincense denoted His death. Yet, it was the gift of myrrh that symbolized His sufferings and what He would have to endure for the sake of mankind. This is why He later became known as a "Man of Sorrows." His only real joy in life came from His abiding relationship with His heavenly Father and obedience to the Father's will.

Jesus "...learned obedience by the things which He suffered" (Hebrews 5:8). Hebrews 2:10 also informs us that Jesus was made "...perfect through sufferings." Are we willing to learn the way of obedience—the way of anointing? Many people today would suggest that because Jesus suffered, we do not have to suffer. They are repeatedly trying to "soften" the demands of discipleship by eliminating the myrrh. Could this be one of the biggest reasons why the Church is lacking a full release of the anointing?

In his book, *WHATEVER HAPPENED TO THE POWER OF GOD*, Michael Brown wrote, "The unspoken—and most probably unconscious—philosophy of many of us has been: We want it all, as long as it costs us nothing! We are willing to make any sacrifice—as long as no hardship is involved. We will gladly persevere in faith—as long as it doesn't take too long. We want to bring God's purposes to birth—as long as there are no labor pains....This way of thinking must become a thing of the past. We need to adjust our mind set. It is time to consider our ways. In the Lord, nothing of real spiritual value comes cheap."[1]

The pathway of discipleship is just as demanding today as it was in the days of Jesus. The "avenue of anointing" is the "way of the cross;" it is the way of suffering, as the "Great Perfumer" carefully blends the "myrrh" into our lives. Without suffering, we will never know the fragrance of His anointing.

THE ESSENCE OF SUFFERING

Three ingredients to the believer's sufferings are essential if we are going to experience the anointing of the Spirit. The first element of suffering involves our own personal trials. The suffering of various trials of our faith is an important stage in our spiritual development. Such hardships are designed by God to mature our faith and prepare us for a greater manifestation of His power and glory. Personal trials can include such things as apparent delays in answers to prayer, personal misfortunes, overcoming temptations and personal weaknesses, and even physical attacks from the enemy who intends to afflict us with some illness.

Smith Wigglesworth, the man who came to be known as the "Apostle of Faith," went through a serious bout with gallstones late in life. His faith in God for healing was severely tested! For three long years he suffered excruciating pain. When informed by a doctor that the only way out of his pain was an operation, Wigglesworth said, "God shall operate." During this period of time, he ministered in the United States, preaching almost every night. Wigglesworth spent his days in bed, was taken by taxi to the meetings each night, and then immediately returned to bed. This continued for weeks. Yet the services were accompanied by **unusual** manifestations of God's healing power. After the stones were eventually passed and he was completely healed, a broken Smith Wigglesworth exhibited a new gentleness, as well as a new anointing, when praying for the sick! This all happened because the myrrh was blended into his life in the apothecary (pharmacy) of God.

The second ingredient of "myrrh" involves suffering on behalf of others. On occasion each of us will be misunderstood, misrepresented and even subjected to verbal abuse. At times, such mistreatment may even come at the hands of other Christians. Yet the Holy Spirit may require us to bear it silently, not allowing us to justify ourselves or our actions. In such cases our heavenly Father is permitting us to suffer in order to teach us how to follow in the footsteps of Jesus by praying on behalf of those who have hurt us.

For those of us who desire to mature in the things of the Spirit, God will insist that we learn to "...help the weak with their weaknesses" (Romans 15:1, New Century Version). Some Christians grow very slowly. Often those who are growing in the Lord find it difficult to understand the immaturity of others and are tempted to become impatient with their doubts, fears, shallow commitment and repeated failures. Patiently suffering such trials on behalf of others not only releases a greater anointing in our lives but also, through our prayers, gives the Lord an opportunity to help lead them into a greater maturity.

The third ingredient of suffering is that which is given to us on behalf of Christ. This is an element of suffering which very few Christians in Western society truly understand. Paul wrote in Philippians 1:29, "For to you it has been granted on behalf of Christ, not only to believe in Him, but also to suffer for His sake." This is the highest form of suffering possible. It is one thing to experience personal hardships or even suffer on behalf of others. However, when we are given the privilege of suffering on behalf of Christ, then the disapproval and disgrace which fell upon Christ also falls upon us; the hatred of the world, as well as the contempt of the religious systems of men, becomes ours; and the mistreatment which was directed against Him also becomes our mistreatment (John 15:18-20). This is what the Apostle Paul meant when speaking of his own sufferings in Colossians 1:24: "I...fill up in my flesh what is lacking in the afflictions of Christ, for the sake of His body, which is the church." If Christ were still on earth, He would continue to suffer at the hands of evil men. Accordingly, He offers us the honor of sharing in His potential sufferings on behalf of His Body, the Church (Philippians 3:10).

Haralan Popov, a Bulgarian pastor, spent thirteen years in Communist prisons for his Christian faith. In the midst of terrible tortures by the Communists as they attempted to force him to deny his faith, the Lord reminded him of Philippians 1:29 and John 15:20-21. The significance of those verses soon became clear to him as he realized that it was not Popov, the tortured man, who was receiving the abuse—it was Jesus being mistreated! Haralan Popov was standing in His place, participating in the sufferings of Christ!

The Word of God clearly says that we as Christians can expect to suffer in this life. "Now if we are children, then we are heirs—heirs of God and co-heirs with Christ, if indeed we share in His sufferings in order that we may also share in His glory" (Romans 8:17, New International Version). Queen Esther shared in the glory of King Ahasuerus because "...she was given the prescribed twelve months of beauty treatments—six months with oil of myrrh, followed by six months with special perfumes and ointments" (Esther 2:12, New Living Translation). Suffering is the rule of the Kingdom of God! A life without seasons of suffering, a life without the "oil of myrrh," will be a life without the beauty and anointing of Christ.

SWEET CINNAMON

Cinnamon came from the bark of the cinnamon shrub and had a distinct fragrant sweetness. The root meaning of the word "cinnamon" is "erect" or "upright." If mixed properly, the holy oil will cause the "anointed" people of God to walk in integrity, holiness and truth. Jesus, the Anointed One, was described as follows: "You have loved righteousness and hated lawlessness; Therefore God, Your God, has anointed You with the oil of gladness more than Your companions" (Hebrews 1:9).

As Christians, we have been given the incredible gift of righteousness through faith in Jesus Christ. His righteousness (right standing before the Father) has actually been counted as ours! Yet if we have truly embraced this precious gift and are walking in its realities, we are going to hate lawlessness and sin just as Jesus did. Righteousness and sin cannot co-exist; one will dominate the other and eventually nullify it!

As the Church, we are reaping the consequences of a defective gospel. In the words of Leonard Ravenhill, "We lack apostolic power because we lack apostolic piety, and we lack apostolic piety because we lack apostolic purity."[2] What kind of message have we proclaimed if it has not produced separation from the world nor bred virtually any hatred of sin? What kind of "plan of salvation" do we present if all we do is apologetically suggest to our hearers that they would be doing Jesus a favor by accepting Him into their hearts? What kind of gospel do we preach when all we tell our listeners is: "Just confess Jesus as Savior and heaven is your home." "Just pray this prayer and it's a done deal." "Just come to the altar; it will only take a few minutes"?

When all we say is "only believe," without calling anyone to true repentance, radical commitment, and a change of lifestyle, what kind of converts do we produce? Where is the evidence of new birth in the lives of so many who have heard our message?

Why is it, that, according to recent statistics, approximately ninety percent of all new converts cannot be found after six months?

"The trouble is the whole 'Accept Christ' attitude is likely to be wrong. It shows Christ applying to us rather than us to Him. It makes Him stand hat-in-hand awaiting our verdict on Him, instead of our kneeling with troubled hearts awaiting His verdict on us. It may even permit us to accept Christ by an impulse of mind or emotions, painlessly, at no loss to our ego and no inconvenience to our usual way of life" (A. W. Tozer).[3]

To be sure, salvation is "by grace through faith" and is a gift from God (Ephesians 2:8). Nothing we can do will add to it. Yet the same grace that brings salvation "...teaches us to say 'No' to ungodliness and worldly passions, and to live self-controlled, upright and godly lives in this present age" (Titus 2:11-12, New International Version). Do we really believe that God's standards have changed? Jesus warned, "Not everyone who says to Me, 'Lord, Lord,' shall enter the kingdom of heaven, but he who does the will of My Father in heaven" (Matthew 7:21). On another occasion, Jesus said, "...If anyone desires to come after Me, let him deny himself, and take up his cross daily, and follow Me" (Luke 9:23). We are admonished in Hebrews 12:14 to "Pursue peace with all men, and holiness, without which no one will see the Lord." In Ephesians 5:3-4, Paul wrote, "But among you there must not be even a hint of sexual immorality, or of any kind of impurity, or of greed, because these are improper for God's holy people. Nor should there be obscenity, foolish talk or coarse joking, which are out of place, but rather thanksgiving" (New International Version). We are challenged in 2 Corinthians 7:1 to "...purify ourselves from everything that contaminates body and spirit, perfecting holiness out of reverence for God" (New International Version).

Some of us, however, have dropped our standards so much that we do not realize how far they have plummeted! How many of us are now watching movies and television programs that would have made us blush just a few short years ago? Do the sexual overtones, not to mention the language, even bother us anymore? How many of us now believe that reading or watching "trash" without feeling any real sting of conviction is a sign of maturity? How many of our children find their heroes and role models in Hollywood rather than in God's Holy Word?

Fun and relaxation are not the issues—compromise and corruption are! How much of our thinking has been shaped by the ungodly influences that surround us? How profoundly has our whole sense of values been shaped by the world's priorities? Research recently done by George Barna and Associates revealed that 71 percent of Americans actually reject the concept of absolute truth. Even more startling is that 62 percent of those who profess to be born-again Christians also believe "...there is no such thing as absolute truth."[4] Yet if there is no absolute truth, then nothing is absolutely true. The entire Christian ethic loses its meaning unless we recognize that God's Word is the supreme authority for all people!

Has peer pressure and the desire to be accepted by others caused us to "soften" our stance so much that black and white issues have now become nothing more than dull gray? Who are we trying to please anyway? As long as we try to win the world by conforming to its ways, we will never experience the power of God in our generation. It is time we allow the Spirit of God to repair our ways! Before we can speak out against the sin in our own land, we must deal with the sin and compromise in our own lives. Before we can call for truth and integrity in others, we must hate the lack of integrity in ourselves.

Some of us Christian leaders need to renounce our Madison Avenue mentality and admit that we have marketed the Gospel for gain and merchandised our ministries for money. Christianity is not big business! The Church is not an industry run by spiritual

124

executives! Ministry is not our road to success, our source of identity or the way to be known and recognized by others.

In wanting to appear "successful," many of us have allowed ourselves to become trapped by "things" and have lost sight of our real calling in Christ. Instead of feeding God's people, many of us find ourselves pleading with them for money in order to keep something afloat that may have never been the will of God in the first place. Ministry means service— giving and not taking—being last and not first! True anointed ministry never exalts or promotes any man.

Some of the Christian music scene has become nothing more than big business as well. Performance has replaced purity. Entertainment has taken the place of worship and anointed ministry. Even "stardom," in some cases, has overshadowed servanthood. We do not need more "superstars"—we need more "super-saints"!

We must all rediscover the true meaning of integrity—a meaning which must include our speech as well as our motives. We spill out thousands of words, yet we rarely grasp the impact of what we say. The exaggeration of truth is commonplace, even though **any** stretching of the truth is a lie in the eyes of God! Promises are made that are never kept. Good intentions are simply not enough because they are still broken promises. We are no better than our word; therefore, it is imperative that we keep our word, even if it personally costs us. "And don't say anything you don't mean. This counsel is embedded deep in our traditions. You only make things worse when you lay down a smoke screen of pious talk, saying, 'I'll pray for you,' and never doing it, or saying, 'God be with you,' and not meaning it. You don't make your words true by embellishing them with religious lace. In making your speech sound more religious, it becomes less true. Just say 'yes' and 'no.' When you manipulate words to get your own way, you go wrong" (Matthew 5:33-37, THE MESSAGE Translation). We must be men and women of integrity! We have no choice! The fragrance of cinnamon will have to envelop us if the power and presence of God are going to be manifested in our lives the way we desire.

We must not only say "no" to ungodliness but also say "yes" to something better! Just saying "no" to sin never works! There must be something more appealing to our hearts to which we can say "yes!" This truth will become more clear to us by looking at the main reason why we sin. None of us sins out of obligation. We sin because we choose to believe that the pleasure it brings is more gratifying than the pleasure obedience brings. The power of temptation is based upon the false premise that sin will make us happier than God can. John Piper so aptly wrote, "Sin is what you do when your heart is not satisfied with God."[5] Therefore, holiness is not attained by just saying "no" to sin; holiness is nourished by an intimate, passionate relationship with God Himself! The only thing that will keep us from being captured by sin is being captivated by Jesus!

SWEET CALAMUS

Calamus was a reed that usually grew in a harsh, difficult clay environment. The word in Hebrew literally means "branch" or "reed." It is also the same word used in Genesis 41:5 for the "stalk" on which heads of grain developed and matured. There was nothing outwardly significant about the calamus, yet it was a channel through which life could flow and produce fruit.

The sweet calamus portrays for us a living, abiding relationship with Jesus, as represented in the parable of the Vine and the branches (John 15). Like the calamus, we find ourselves in a hostile environment that can make it extremely hard to produce life. Unless we continually abide in the Vine and maintain an ongoing relationship with Christ, we will never grow or flourish. However, if we nurture our intimacy with the Lord, nothing in our environment can keep us from bearing fruit and becoming "channels" of the anointing. We can be placed in the worst circumstances, experience the harshest surroundings and still thrive in the service of God!

To some John the Baptist appeared to be nothing more than a "reed shaken by the wind" (Matthew 11:7); however, this "reed," though surrounded by a hostile environment, struck fear in the heart of wicked Herod and caused all of society to tremble!

At the trial of Jesus, soldiers not only put a crown of thorns upon His head but also placed a flimsy "reed" in His hand and mocked Him as the "King of the Jews." Yet in the wisdom of God, this "reed" became the royal scepter in the hand of Christ that would later illustrate His absolute rule and dominion over all creation!

In this hour, God is looking for those who are willing to be nothing more than a "reed" through which His life and anointing can flow. While these individuals may appear to be insignificant, they will become channels of God's presence and power. By consistently yielding to the work of the Holy Spirit, even during times of being battered and beaten, they will eventually become "stalks of strength," giving support to those around them.

Years ago, a missionary to Africa was asked to tour the upper Nile to explore the possibilities of making paper for the world's use from the vast areas of papyrus found in that region. While on the trip, he came across a group of people who lived on the banks of Lake Tsana in Ethiopia. He discovered that these natives built large canoe-like boats out of papyrus. Of this experience he later wrote,

> They select long reeds and cut off their feathery heads; then they bind them together into a great bundle with a pointed prow [bow of the boat] and a wide, depressed-in-the-center body. Every foot or so there is a binding rope. As those reeds are very slippery they must be bruised by striking at the

places where the strongest ties must come so that the rope can compress that pithy center and take a firm grip on the outside of the reed. This is only necessary for the outer layer of reeds that hold the whole together. When they are tightly tied, the inner layers will not slip out. The ones that have been bruised will carry the constricting rope so that it does not slip off and let the boat sink or disintegrate.

How often, in Christian experience, it is the persons who have had the worst buffetings who really hold the vessel together and are the greatest sources of strength to the church. The bruising is not for punishment but for strengthening. It is said of Christ, 'He was bruised for our iniquities: the chastisement of our peace was upon Him; and with His stripes we are healed' (Isaiah 53:5). The Lord may bruise us so that we may help others, may keep others from sinking.[6]

CASSIA

Cassia, like cinnamon, came from the bark of a shrub. It grew at high altitudes and produced a small purple flower. The root meaning of the word is "shriveled" and comes from the same root as the word "bowed down" mentioned in Genesis 24:26, where Abraham's servant bowed his head and worshipped the Lord in reverence and humility.

Cassia reminds us of the nature of true worship. True worship must be seen primarily as an attitude of the heart and not just an act we perform during church services. In fact, the first reference in the Bible to the word "worship" involved the offering up of Isaac, Abraham's son, on the altar of Mount Moriah (Genesis 22:1-14).

True worship always leads to our giving everything in absolute surrender to the lordship of Christ. It means that our ambitions, desires, hopes, dreams, wills, our very lives—all must be given to Jesus! When King Jesus invades the "kingdom" of our lives, He requires unconditional surrender (Luke 14:31-33). Only one "king" can rule our lives; either "self " or Christ will rule on the throne of our hearts. There is no other alternative! We cannot know Jesus as Savior without knowing Him as the Lord of our lives. This truth is reinforced by the fact that the word "Savior" is found only 24 times in the New Testament while the word "Lord" is mentioned 433 times.

In the book of Joshua, we find that just before Israel's attack on the city of Jericho, Joshua had an experience that forever changed his life. We read in Joshua 5:13-15, "And it came to pass, when Joshua was by Jericho, that he lifted his eyes and looked, and behold, a Man stood opposite him with His sword drawn in His hand. And Joshua went to Him and said to Him, 'Are You for us or for our adversaries?' So He said, 'No, but as Commander of the army of the Lord I have now come.' And Joshua fell on his face to the earth and worshiped, and said to Him, 'What does my Lord say to His servant?' Then the Commander of the Lord's army said to Joshua, 'Take your sandal off your foot, for the place where you stand is holy.' And Joshua did so." Now Joshua did not have an encounter with just any ordinary angel. This was none other than the Pre-Incarnate Christ, for when Joshua asked Him, "Are You for us or for our adversaries?" the Lord said, "No, but as Commander of the army of the Lord I have now come" (vs.13b-14a). In other words, Jesus said to Joshua, "I have not come to take sides; I have come to take over!"

When the Commander of the armies of Heaven invades our lives, He does not come to take sides with "self;" neither does He

129

come to share the throne of our hearts with another. He comes to take over! He requires complete surrender on our part. Yet what is absolute surrender?

First of all, absolute surrender is an absolute lack of resistance. Total surrender is not something we do; it is an attitude of the heart in which we do not resist the Lord when He comes to take control of every area of our lives. Absolute surrender involves humbly submitting to His work as He removes from our hearts those things that displease Him and defy His authority. It includes yielding to His Spirit to such a degree that we do not oppose Him when He would desire to instruct us about something, correct us or mature us by allowing our faith to be tested.

Absolute surrender is a passive state; it is an absence of rebellion to the lordship of Christ. It is not something we strive to do. None of us tries to breathe. Neither do we, as parents, try to love our children. Likewise, none of us as Christians are called to try to surrender to Christ. Jesus did not try to yield to the will of His Father; He simply did not resist it. Each of us can do the same! We need to allow the Holy Spirit to bring us to the place where we are willing to surrender everything without reservation to the Lord so that He can work His perfect will both in and through us.

Absolute surrender is not only a lack of resistance but also a lack of any expression of self-will. The yielding of our lives to the lordship of Christ requires complete consecration of our wills to the Spirit of God. Jesus Himself instructed us to pray, "...Our Father in heaven, hallowed be Your name. Your kingdom come. Your will be done on earth as it is in heaven" (Matthew 6:9-10). For the will of God to be accomplished on earth, it must happen through those of us who surrender our wills to the Lord.

The unwillingness to surrender our wills and bring them into agreement with God's has been the cause of many of our problems.

There is real danger in a will which is not fully surrendered to Christ, because any part of a will that is not yielded to Him is open for Satan to influence and control. We must remember that self-will culminated in the fall of man into sin with all of its hideous consequences. Therefore, any part of our will that is not committed to the Lord is sinful self-will and is either under our control or the influence of Satan. In either case, self-will is a defiant resistance to the lordship of Christ in our lives.

This truth is vividly illustrated for us by looking to the life of the Apostle Peter. In Acts 10:9-15, we find that "...Peter went up on the housetop to pray, about the sixth hour. Then he became very hungry and wanted to eat; but while they made ready, he fell into a trance and saw heaven opened and an object like a great sheet bound at the four corners, descending to him and let down to the earth. In it were all kinds of four-footed animals of the earth, wild beasts, creeping things, and birds of the air. And a voice came to him, 'Rise, Peter; kill and eat.' But Peter said, 'Not so, Lord! For I have never eaten anything common or unclean.' And a voice spoke to him again the second time, 'What God has cleansed you must not call common.'"

Although we are certainly not trying to criticize Peter, we must understand that his response to the Lord's voice while in the trance was a complete contradiction in terms. What Peter heard and was instructed to do would have been traumatic for any conservative Jew. No wonder he reacted the way he did. Yet he clearly did not realize the significance of what he had said. When Peter answered, "Not so, Lord," his reply was completely inconsistent with his testimony. How could Peter consider Jesus to be the Lord of his life and still say, "Not so, Lord"? To be sure, Peter's response was one of shock and alarm, but the message for us rings loud and clear! How can Jesus be the Savior and Lord of our lives if we are continually saying to Him by our attitudes and actions, "Not so, Lord"?

Some of us may feel that to lose our self-will would mean the loss of the freedom of our will. However, the total commitment of our will to the Holy Spirit is not the surrender of its free expression but the surrender of its **selfish, independent** exercise, bringing it into agreement with the Lord's. The will that is not in agreement with God's is not really free because in such a condition it is only free to choose how it will oppose God's will and purpose. While God never destroys our power of choice, He does require that we surrender our selfish will and bring it into harmony with His.

This is what Jesus meant in Luke 9:23 when He said, "...If anyone desires to come after Me, let him deny himself, and take up his cross daily, and follow Me." The denial of self does not mean that we are to deny ourselves "things." It means to deny **ourselves.** The denial of self is God-centered; self-denial is self-centered. The denial of self means that we count ourselves as dead so that Christ can live and reign in us. This fundamental truth was reinforced by the Apostle Paul when he wrote in Galatians 2:20, "I have been crucified with Christ; it is no longer I who live, but Christ lives in me...." Christ can only rule our lives to the degree we consider ourselves dead.

Our lives belong to King Jesus, along with everything they include. Nevertheless, if we are not willing to continually deny ourselves and take up our crosses daily, we are in effect saying, "Jesus, You bought me but You cannot have me." We must not be like those who want the power of God but are not willing to take the posture of true worship before the Lord. We dare not be like those who desire signs without surrender. Instead, let us be those who continue to grow in the high altitude of holy surrender where our lives can blossom and bring honor to our King!

OLIVE OIL

Throughout Scripture olive oil has often been used as a symbol of the Holy Spirit. Olive oil was the ingredient that held all of the spices together. It was produced by the crushing of olive berries between roughly hewn stones.

Just prior to His crucifixion, Jesus was in a garden called Gethsemane, wrestling with the stark reality of His impending death. It is significant that the word "Gethsemane" means "oil press." Through the breaking and eventual crushing that Jesus experienced, the holy oil of the Spirit was poured out for suffering humanity.

When the word "broken" is found in Scripture, it is usually accompanied by the word "contrite." (See Psalm 34:18; Psalm 51:17; Isaiah 57:15 and Isaiah 66:2.) The word "contrite" means "crushed" or "crumbled." The English equivalent of the same word means "crushed to powder." These two words are often found together to emphasize for us the difference between occasionally experiencing the breaking process and being so broken that our self-will can never be mended again. For example, a vase can fall from a shelf and be broken, but if the break is not too severe, it can usually be put back together. However if it is repeatedly broken, some of the pieces will become like powder, and the vase will never be able to be reconstructed.

Self-will has always been God's greatest competitor for our love and affections. This issue stands at the heart of the very first commandment given to Moses. In Exodus 20:3, the Lord said, "You shall have no other gods before Me." Our Father has such a holy jealousy for our love that He will not allow anyone or anything to come before Him. In His great love and mercy, He continually leads us back to Gethsemane. Each encounter with the pressure of God's "oil press" is not only intended to crush our self-will with its pride and independence but also to allow the anointing oil of God's Spirit to be fully released in our lives.

How many times have we made attempts in our own strength to grow in the character of Christ only to fail miserably? How many times have we made "spiritual New Year's resolutions" only to never act upon them? The only way we can experience the anointing, the beauty and the holiness of Jesus is to allow the Holy Spirit to blend the various ingredients of His grace into our lives.

The "Great Perfumer" is the only One who knows this wonderful "art." Therefore, we must be willing to undergo the process through which the anointing oil can flow out of our lives to others. The fragrance of the anointing can only be released in us as we are broken and crushed by the loving activity of the Holy Spirit. Our Father always leads us this way to prepare us for a richer, purer anointing!

In full and glad surrender
I give myself to Thee;
Thine utterly and only,
And evermore to be.

O, Son of God, who lov'st me,
I will be Thine alone,
And all I have, and all I am
Shall henceforth be Thine own.

O, come and reign, Lord Jesus;
Rule over everything;
And KEEP ME always loyal,
And true to Thee, my King.

Frances R. Havergal

* Emphasis added

Chapter Nine
SONS OF FRESH OIL (TWO)

The anointing oil was so sacred to the Lord that He gave instructions to Moses for its protection. Restrictions and prohibitions were placed upon its use that still apply to us today. In Exodus 30:31-33 we read, "And thou shalt speak unto the children of Israel, saying, This shall be an holy anointing oil unto me throughout your generations. Upon man's flesh shall it not be poured, neither shall ye make any other like it, after the composition of it: it is holy, and it shall be holy unto you. Whosoever compoundeth any like it, or whosoever putteth any of it upon a stranger, shall even be cut off from his people" (King James Version).

THE ANOINTING OIL IS NOT FOR THE FLESH

God will not pour out His anointing upon human carnality! Although Christians will do fleshly things, the Scriptures are opposed to carnal lifestyles. There is no such thing as "carnal Christianity!" We are deceived if we think that we can know Jesus as Savior and still continue in sin. Nowhere in the Word of God is the practice of sin condoned. 1 John 2:1 informs us that "...if anyone sins, we have an Advocate with the Father, Jesus Christ the righteous." Notice, this verse says **if** we sin, not **when** we sin.

Someone once wrote, "Christians seem to me to divide into two groups these days: the first lot don't think sin matters very much anyway, and the second know perfectly well that it does, but still can't kick the habit." Many Christians cling to the erroneous idea that even after conversion, every Christian still has an old sinful nature from which he cannot escape until death. The "two natures theory" has often been used as an excuse for justifying sin, defeat and mediocrity in the lives of believers. Embracing this unscriptural teaching enables many professing Christians to reconcile the distinct contradiction between their carnal lifestyles and the absolute standards of Scripture. They can excuse their attitudes and actions by pointing out that it was their sinful nature that lost its temper, gave in to lustful thoughts or lied or cheated. However, in 1 John 3:9-10 we read, "Those who have been born into God's family do not sin, because God's life is in them. So they can't **keep on** sinning, because they have been born of God" (New Living Translation).*

Moreover, the Word of God teaches that a man in his unsaved state does not simply possess a sinful nature but that he himself is sinful. A man's nature is not some intangible thing which cannot be explained; in essence, his nature is the man himself. Every man is fallen, corrupt, sinful and alienated from God. When an individual is born again, he is cleansed, changed and made spiritually alive. In fact, the word "nature," as it relates to a man's personality, is found only once in the New Testament. Paul wrote in Ephesians 2: 1-3, "And you he made alive, who were dead in trespasses and sins, in which you once walked according to the course of this world, according to the prince of the power of the air, the spirit who now works in the sons of disobedience, among whom also we all once conducted ourselves in the lusts of our flesh, fulfilling the desires of the flesh and of the mind, and were by nature children of wrath, just as the others."

It is significant that Paul said in verse one that we were made alive by God, not just some part of our nature. He went on to inform us that we "were by nature children of wrath." By using this phrase, Paul was clearly implying that we are now new creatures in

Christ. God no longer speaks of us as "sinners," but calls us "sons" instead. The Scriptures instruct us that we have been cleansed, washed, sanctified (set apart for holy service) and freed from sin.

Furthermore, when Paul referred to the old and new man in his writings, he was not advocating that the believer has two natures. The terms "old man" and "new man" are used figuratively to speak of what we were in Adam and have now become in Christ. In Romans 6:6, we are informed "...that our old man was crucified with Him." The New Living Translation says, "Our old sinful selves were crucified with Christ so that sin might lose its power in our lives. We are no longer slaves to sin." As a result, we have been "...set free from the power of sin" (v.7). When Paul wrote in Ephesians 4:22-24, "that you put off, concerning your former conduct, the old man which grows corrupt according to the deceitful lusts, and be renewed in the spirit of your mind, and that you put on the new man which was created according to God, in righteousness and true holiness," he was challenging Christians not to live according to their pre-salvation attitudes, outlook and values. Paul further reinforced this truth in Romans 6:11-12, by saying, "...reckon [consider] yourselves to be dead indeed to sin, but alive to God in Christ Jesus our Lord. Therefore do not let sin reign in your mortal body, that you should obey it in its lusts."

In addressing the Church at Corinth, Paul did refer to the believers as carnal. In fact, he went so far as to suggest that they were spiritual babies when he wrote, "...I fed you with milk and not with solid food; for until now you were not able to receive it, and even now you are still not able; for you are still carnal. For where there are envy, strife, and divisions among you, are you not carnal and behaving like mere men?" (1 Corinthians 3:1-3). Yet the language of these verses does not imply that Paul endorsed their carnal, fleshly behavior! He was actually trying to persuade them to act like men and women of the Spirit. The irony of these verses lies in the fact that the Corinthians, who thought of themselves as spiritually mature people, were acting and thinking just as they did before they came to Christ.

At this point, the question might arise, "But what about the intense, emotional story of Paul's own internal struggle mentioned in Romans 7:13-25? Doesn't this passage seem to indicate that Paul himself struggled continually with the pull of his old, sinful nature?" If we take this passage out of context, we might come to that conclusion. However, if we study the surrounding verses, we will come away with a more accurate perspective of what Paul was actually addressing.

The theme woven throughout these verses deals with the place of the Law in the life of the Christian. In verses one through six, Paul made it clear that the believer has no relationship to the Law at all. According to verse six, "...we have been released from the law, for we died with Christ, and we are no longer captive to its power. Now we can really serve God, not in the old way by obeying the letter of the law, but in the new way, by the Spirit" (New Living Translation). However, Paul was not suggesting that the Law was unholy and evil; it simply was helpless to empower individuals to do what it required.

In this passage Paul described what it was like to live under the Law before experiencing Christ and the indwelling Holy Spirit. The language Paul used in these verses expresses the intensity of his feelings toward the futility of the Law to do anything about the problem of sin! Those under the Law were incapable of doing the things it demanded. For the individual under law, who had not experienced the gift of the Spirit, sin was clearly the stronger power. The picture Paul painted throughout the seventh chapter of Romans is absolutely irreconcilable with his view of life in Christ, empowered by the Holy Spirit! Notice the contrast between verses 7-25 and Romans 8:1-2; it is like the difference between night and day! Romans 8:1-2 is God's answer to the cry of the distressed person struggling with sin, as mentioned in Romans 7:24. Paul declared emphatically that there is no condemnation to those of us who are in Christ. The judgment we all deserved has been removed through His death. We now live by a new "law," that of the Spirit of life in Christ Jesus. What the Law could not do, Christ has legally done for us. The bondage of sin has been broken! The Holy Spirit, in turn, has come to enable us to experience victory over sin as we yield to His power in our lives (Romans 8:3-4).

Many of us, however, feel so helpless because of our own personal failures that this seems far too unrealistic. Because the text in Romans 7 describes something we know all too well, we have adopted views that are compatible with our experience instead of adjusting our beliefs to the complete revelation of Scripture. Many of us have even taken comfort in believing that Paul was addressing the internal struggle between the old and new natures when he wrote in Galatians 5:16-17, "...Walk in [by] the Spirit, and you shall not fulfill the lust of the flesh. For the flesh lusts against the Spirit, and the Spirit against the flesh; and these are contrary to one another, so that you do not do the things that you wish."

Yet, what did Paul actually mean by the term "flesh?" The basic meaning of the word "flesh" in Scripture is the material or physical body. Paul, however, seldom used the Greek word for "flesh" to refer to the physical body. Although he used the term to refer to our humanity in some form or another (Romans 1:3; 4:1; 1 Corinthians 10:18; Galatians 2:20), more often than not Paul used the concept of flesh and spirit in a moral and ethical sense. This concept lay at the heart of his message throughout his writings. To Paul, the flesh signified the unregenerate state with its sin and corruption, as was vividly depicted in his contrast between life "according to the flesh" as opposed to life "according to the Spirit" (Romans 7-8). The carnal or fleshly mind symbolized the unregenerate mind (Romans 8:5-7). The unsaved were said to be "in the flesh [and] cannot please God" (v.8), while the Christian was "not in the flesh, but in the Spirit" (v.9).

With this background in mind, we can see that Paul was not teaching the doctrine of two natures in Galatians 5:16-17. He was not talking about some continuous, internal struggle of the believer but, instead, giving in to the ungodly behavior of the past. Walking in the Spirit is incompatible with living according to the flesh, because the two are in complete opposition to each other. The Holy Spirit resists the old way of living and empowers us to live in entirely new freedom in Christ.

However, the Christian life is not a walk down "Easy Street." As God's people, we can still be overtaken by faults (Galatians 6:1). Although our bodies are not sinful in themselves, we do have natural appetites and desires that are vulnerable to temptation. We live in a world with many attractions and enticements. We also have minds that are susceptible to the suggestions of the Enemy as he continually attempts to trap us through ungodly thoughts.

Furthermore, we are still learning how to walk by the Spirit and yield to His work in our lives. We are in constant need of experiencing God's grace and forgiveness. Yet this does not mean we are to accept living in sin as inevitable, as though the Holy Spirit were not capable of empowering us to overcome. We have been invaded by God Himself! Since His goal is to conform us thoroughly to the likeness of Christ, the Spirit of God will never anoint a life that is repeatedly given over to carnality.

When Noah wanted to discover whether the flood waters had receded from the face of the earth, he sent out a raven, hoping the bird would return with evidence that it was safe to leave the Ark. The jet-black bird soared out across the waters, but Noah never saw him again. The flesh-eating bird naturally did not want to return to the Ark with its restricted feeding conditions. An incredible banquet was waiting for him outside! An entire civilization had died!

After waiting in vain for the raven to return, Noah released a dove, hoping for better results this time. And he got them. The dove was not a flesh-eater; the death and decay were repulsive to all her instincts. On her graceful wings she soared past every rotting carcass and eventually returned to Noah.

Even today, the precious dove of the Holy Spirit wings His way past that which is fleshly. The stench of carnality is still repulsive to all His divine instincts.

THERE MUST NOT BE ANY SUBSTITUTE ANOINTING

Over the years, a growing number of professing Christians have developed an appetite for "spiritual hype." We enjoy and even delight in the sensational packaging of professional ministries and overlook the absence of a true anointing of the Spirit. A minister's success is now measured by his popularity or the size of his budget, instead of being gauged by his Christlikeness and the presence of God that resides upon him. Some of us even like the entertainment value of meetings where men and women strut their "stuff," boast of great gifts and have the ability to whip up a crowd.

Yet despite the marketing and promotion, there is little real substance to the messages or the manifestations being heralded. What a stark contrast in comparison to the ministry of Jonathan Edwards who, although he read his sermons in a dull monotone, walked in such divine authority that, at times when he spoke, people literally trembled under holy conviction!

When the godly Scottish preacher Robert Murray McCheyne entered the pulpit to preach, people would begin to weep and fall under conviction without McCheyne ever saying a word. The difference in this man's ministry that caused people to be so deeply affected stemmed from the hours that McCheyne spent alone with

God in prayer. He would reportedly come directly from the presence of the Lord, and the Holy Spirit would fall upon the people.

Where is the glory of God today? Where is the presence of God that causes people to tremble under holy conviction? Where is the sense of awe that leaves people speechless because of the miracles done in their midst? When men such as John G. Lake, Stephen Jeffreys and Smith Wigglesworth conducted healing services years ago, wheelchairs were emptied, blind eyes were opened, and tumors disappeared. Some people were even knocked to the ground by the power of God. In our meetings today, people apparently fall under the power of God, yet far too many walk away sick and hurting. Where are all the verifiable healings? Why is there so much excitement over people falling on the floor? Why all the hype?

We can compare what we see today with what P. J. Madden shared in his book, *THE WIGGLESWORTH STANDARD.* In relating an incident that took place under the ministry of Wigglesworth, Mr. Madden wrote,

> While staying in the home of a curate of the local Church of England, [Wigglesworth] and the curate were sitting together talking after supper. No doubt the subject of their conversation was that the poor fellow had no legs. Artificial limbs in those days were unlike the sophisticated limbs of today.
>
> Wigglesworth said to the man quite suddenly (which he often did when ministering in cases like this), "Go and get a pair of new shoes in the morning."
>
> The poor fellow thought it was some kind of joke. However, after Wigglesworth and the curate had retired to their respective rooms for the night, God said to the curate, "Do as My servant hath said." What a designation for any person—My servant!

God was identifying Himself with Wigglesworth.

There was no more sleep for the man that night. He rose up early, went downtown, and stood waiting for the shoe shop to open. The manager eventually arrived and opened the shop for business.

The curate went in and sat down. Presently an assistant came and said, "Good morning, sir. Can I help you?"

The man said, "Yes, would you get me a pair of shoes, please."

"Yes, sir. Size and color?"

The curate hesitated. The assistant then saw his condition and said, "Sorry, sir. We can't help you."

"It's all right, young man. But I do want a pair of shoes. Size 8, color black."

The assistant went to get the requested shoes. A few minutes later he returned and handed them to the man. The man put one stump into a shoe, and instantly a foot and leg formed! Then the same thing happened with the other leg!

He walked out of that shop, not only with a new pair of shoes, but also with a new pair of legs!

Wigglesworth was not surprised. He had expected the result. He often made remarks like this: "As far as God is concerned, there is no difference between forming a limb and healing a broken bone."[1]

THE NEED FOR A REALITY CHECK

There has never been a time like today when so little power has been marketed as being so great! We have substituted programs for power, sensationalism for signs, hype for healing and methods for miracles. Certain ministers have even suggested that it is better to have a little "strange fire" than to have no fire at all. Yet, have we forgotten what happened to Nadab and Abihu (Leviticus 10:1-2)? Do we not understood that the word "antichrist" not only means "against Christ" but also means "instead of Christ?" Have we never grasped the fact that the word "Christ" means "Anointed One" and that anything used as a substitute for a true anointing of the Spirit is really "antichrist" in nature?

The point of this message is not to be critical! However, it is high time all of us seek God for the real thing! We need His holy presence to bring true conviction of sin. We need a holy passion that will awaken us to real miracles. It may be more costly, but there is nothing comparable to God's holy anointing! In the words of John G. Lake, "We may never get one half or one quarter of the way toward the ideal. But never try to degrade God's purpose and bring it down to your level. But by the grace of God put the standard up there where Jesus put it, and then get as near it as you can."[2]

THE ANOINTING IS NOT FOR THE STRANGER

In Ezekiel 44:7,9, we find God grieving over the sins of the house of Israel. In chiding the priests for their rebellion, He said to them, "...ye have brought into my sanctuary strangers, uncircumcised in heart and uncircumcised in flesh, to be in my sanctuary, to pollute it, even my house, when you offer my bread, the fat and the blood, and they have broken my covenant because of all your abominations...Thus saith the Lord God; No stranger, uncircumcised in heart or uncircumcised in flesh, shall enter into my sanctuary, of any stranger that is among the children of Israel" (King James Version).

Every covenant God made with man was sealed by a sign that was to serve as a continual reminder of His faithfulness. For example, when God entered into covenant with Noah, He gave the rainbow as a sign that He would never again destroy the earth with water. Every time Noah looked at a rainbow, it reminded him of God's faithfulness to give him an inheritance as well as a hope for the future.

When God entered into covenant with Abraham, He said, "...and you shall be circumcised in the flesh of your foreskins, and it shall be a sign of the covenant between Me and you" (Genesis 17:11). Circumcision was to be the lasting sign of the covenant to remind Abraham of the guarantee of God's promises.

Circumcision was also an outward symbol which indicated the need for cleansing. Through the cutting away of the male foreskin, the Lord distinctly revealed to His people that without purification there could be no covenant between a holy God and an unholy people.

Furthermore, circumcision signified the actual process of cleansing which was essential for walking in covenant with God. The corruption of the flesh had to be removed. Whatever defiled the people of God had to be cut away.

We must understand that circumcision under the Old Covenant was actually a picture of the work of the Holy Spirit in the lives of those who would later come to Christ under the New Covenant. Paul declared in Romans 2:28-29, "For he is not a Jew who is one outwardly; neither is circumcision that which is outward in the flesh...he is a Jew who is one inwardly; and circumcision is that which is of the heart, by the Spirit...." (New American Standard

Version). The circumcision of the New Covenant is initially a cleansing work of the heart by the Spirit of God. Paul further reinforced this truth in Colossians 2:11: "When you came to Christ, you were circumcised, but not by a physical procedure. It was a spiritual procedure—the cutting away of your sinful nature" (New Living Translation).

While circumcision of the heart is necessary for initial participation in the New Covenant, it also symbolizes the need and process of continual purification. A recurring inner work of cleansing by the Spirit is essential for a life of obedience and wholehearted love and devotion to God. This requirement of obedience was not done away with in the New Covenant. However, God has promised always to provide the means for us to obey through the power of His Spirit. Peter said it best when he wrote that it is "...by the sanctifying work of the Spirit, that you may obey Jesus Christ and be sprinkled by His blood...." (1 Peter 1:2, New American Standard Version).

Therefore, to walk in covenant with God, we must allow the Holy Spirit to repeatedly cut away the sins of the flesh from our hearts. We cannot walk in covenant and live for ourselves. We can no longer pursue our own will and passions. We can no longer live for the desires of the flesh. Paul wrote, "For if you live according to the flesh you will die; but if by the Spirit you put to death the deeds of the body [lusts of the flesh], you will live. For as many as are led by the Spirit of God, these are sons of God" (Romans 8:13-14). Clearly, the sins of the flesh can only be put to death as we yield to the Spirit's work in our hearts.

To reject this circumcision of heart is to reject the Holy Spirit and is proof one is not walking in covenant with God. No wonder God said that whoever put the anointing oil on a stranger would be cut off. The "stranger," according to Ezekiel 44:7,9, was the man who was uncircumcised in heart. He not only symbolized the foreigner who was outside the nation of Israel but all those who were

"...circumcised and yet uncircumcised" (Jeremiah 9:25, New American Standard Version).

When Moses instructed the children of Israel about circumcision, he knew the Lord was not wanting just an outward obedience. Accordingly, Moses told the people that "...the Lord your God will circumcise your heart and the heart of your descendants, to love the Lord your God with all your heart and with all your soul, that you may live" (Deuteronomy 30:6). The obedience God desired was to be the response of a life fully devoted to Him. Since He expected His people to fear Him, walk in all His ways and lovingly serve Him with all their hearts (Deuteronomy 10:12), the Lord warned them: "...circumcise the foreskin of your heart, and be stiffnecked no longer " (v.16). To be stiffnecked meant to refuse the circumcision of the heart and the cleansing work of God's Spirit.

This same truth is reiterated in Acts 7, when Stephen, addressing the religious leaders of his day, said to them, "...our fathers were unwilling to be obedient...and in their hearts turned back to Egypt [the world]...You men who are stiffnecked and uncircumcised in heart and ears are always resisting the Holy Spirit; you are doing just as your fathers did" (vs.39, 51, New American Standard Version). These verses again make it clear that an uncircumcised heart is one that continually resists the cleansing work of the Spirit and turns back to the lusts of the world and the flesh.

Nothing grieves the heart of God more than those who resist the Spirit's work of circumcision and refuse to respond to His conviction! They have broken covenant with Him and can only look forward to His holy wrath! Hebrews 10:26-31 puts it in even stronger terms: "Dear friends, if we deliberately continue sinning after we have received a full knowledge of the truth, there is no other sacrifice that will cover these sins. There will be nothing to look forward to but the terrible expectation of God's judgment and the raging fire that will consume his enemies. Anyone who refused to obey the law of Moses was put to death without mercy on the testimony of two or three witnesses. Think how much more terrible the punishment will be for those who have trampled on the Son of God and have treated the blood of the covenant as if it were common and unholy. Such people have insulted and enraged the Holy Spirit who brings God's mercy to his people. For we know the one who said, 'I will take vengeance. I will repay those who deserve it.' He also said, 'The Lord will judge his own people.' It is a terrible thing to fall into the hands of the living God" (New Living Translation).

God's demands have not changed under the New Covenant. His requirements did not diminish with the coming of Christ and His work of grace. The warnings throughout Scripture still ring loud and clear—mere lip-service and outward obedience will never do! The "stranger" who is uncircumcised in heart and continues in sin will be cut off. The disobedient in heart will never bear the fragrance of God's holy anointing!

THE ANOINTING OIL IS HOLY

When the holy anointing oil was poured upon an individual, it was impossible for that person not to become immediately distinguishable from others by a unique fragrance. The aroma of the spices was delightful and unmistakable.

If the anointing of the Holy Spirit means anything at all, it means that those individuals truly filled with the Spirit will manifest the unmistakable fragrance of holiness, humility and love. They will not be arrogant, greedy, jealous, proud or vulgar. They will be separate and distinct from those who claim to be Spirit-filled and yet split churches and sow discord among believers. Truly Spirit-filled people will not be like those whose ambitions drive them to build their own kingdoms and seek a place in the limelight. They will be noticeably different because the anointing is holy and everything it touches becomes holy!

In Acts 6, we are introduced to a man named Stephen who was so filled with the Spirit that great signs and wonders were done through his ministry (v.8). Even though Stephen was just a newly appointed deacon in the Early Church, his life was so full of God that everywhere he went the anointing spilled over onto those with whom he came in contact.

Certain individuals, however, from the synagogue of the Freedmen sought to argue and debate with Stephen but were overcome by the wisdom and the spirit with which he spoke. Humiliated and enraged, these men plotted Stephen's death and had him arrested and brought before the council under false charges (vs.9-14). From that moment on, there would be no justice for Stephen; he was as good as dead!

Yet as Stephen stood before the council for the last time, something took place that was "out of this world!" His face became as bright as an angel's (v.15). Although the dark shadows of hatred and death swirled around him, the celestial beauty of Christ radiated in pure light from his face. Even when dying from the savage pounding of the stones against him, Stephen was still able to pray, "Lord, do not charge them with this sin" (Acts 7:60).

The fragrance of that holy occasion must have struck at the very heart of a young man named Saul who held the garments of those who were stoning Stephen. Surely before his dramatic confrontation with Jesus on the Damascus Road, the waking moments of Saul's life must have been haunted by the heavenly expression discernible even through all of the blood on Stephen's face. Saul (who later became known as Paul) never forgot the unmistakable aroma that rested on the life of that holy, anointed, magnificent man!

A 20th century example of this reality was clearly demonstrated in the life and ministry of Smith Wigglesworth. On one occasion he shared, "I remember one time stepping out of a railroad car to wash my hands. I had a season of prayer, and the Lord just filled me to overflowing with His love. I was going to a convention in Ireland, and I could not get there fast enough. As I returned, I believe that the Spirit of the Lord was so heavily upon me that my face must have shone. (No man can tell himself when the Spirit transforms his very countenance.) There were two clerical men sitting together, and as I got into the carriage again, one of them cried out, 'You convict me of sin.' Within three minutes everyone in the car was crying to God for salvation. This thing has happened many times in my life. It is this ministration of the Spirit that Paul speaks of [2 Cor.3], this filling of the Spirit that will make your life effective so that even the people in the stores where you trade will want to leave your presence because they are brought under conviction."[3]

A LIMITLESS SUPPLY OF OIL

For those of us who are willing to walk in the restrictions of the anointing, an inexhaustible supply of oil is promised to us! In the vision God gave to Zechariah at the time of the building of the second temple, the prophet saw "...a lampstand of solid gold with a bowl on top of it, and on the stand seven lamps with seven pipes to the seven lamps. Two olive trees are by it, one at the right of the bowl and the other at its left" (Zechariah 4:2-3). Zechariah then asked the angel who was talking with him, "...What are these two olive trees—at the right of the lampstand and at its left?....What are these two olive branches that drip into the receptacles of the two gold pipes from which the golden oil drains?" The angel answered Zechariah, "...These are the two anointed ones [literally, sons of fresh oil], who are standing by the Lord of the whole earth" (vs.11,12,14).

In this vision, Zechariah saw a lampstand joined to two olive trees. God showed him that the olive trees were the "sons of fresh oil," the anointed ones. Through these "anointed ones" an inexhaustible supply of oil would be provided for the lamp of God. The lampstand in the temple stood for the true light of revelation given to the people of God. Joshua, the High Priest, and Zerubbabel were represented by the two olive trees seen in Zechariah's vision. They were God's ministers to the people. In representing both the priesthood and the kingship, they would be God's source of revelation and light to the world.

In this passage, we find a wonderful "type" of what is available to those who will surrender everything to Christ just for the prize of knowing Him. God wants to manifest in us the same anointing that He gave to Jesus (1 John 2:27). He wants us to be so joined to His Son, the "Anointed One," that a limitless supply of oil will flow through us to others. As kings and priests of the New Covenant, we are to be God's source of light and revelation to a world groping in darkness. God is calling each of us to be "sons of fresh oil!"

"God makes His ministers a flame of fire. Am I ignitable? God, deliver me from the dread asbestos of 'other things.' Saturate me with the oil of Thy Spirit that I may be a flame. Make me Thy fuel, Flame of God."

Jim Eliot — martyred by the Auca Indians

* Emphasis added

ENDNOTES

Introduction

1. Quoted by W. B. Knight, *3000 Illustrations for Christian Service* (Grand Rapids, MI: Eerdmans, 1957) 566.

2. Arthur Skevington Wood, *Baptised with Fire* (London: Pickering & Inglis, 1981) 175.

3. H. P. Barker, *Windows in Words* (London: Pickering & Inglis, 1954) 130.

Chapter One

1. Colin C. Whittaker, *Great Revivals* (Springfield, MO: Gospel Publishing House, 1986) 50.

2. John Wesley, *Journals of John Wesley* (Epworth Press, 1938) 148.

3. Wesley 475-476.

4. Stephen F. Olford, *Heart Cry for Revival* (Grand Rapids, MI: Zondervan, 1970) 31.

5. Whittaker 88.

6. Edwin J. Orr, *The Fervent Prayer: The Worldwide Impact of the Great Awakening of 1858* (Chicago: Moody Press, 1974) 51.

7. Olford 103-104.

8. Whittaker 182-183.

9. Whittaker 187-188.

10. James A.. Stewart, *Opened Windows* (Alexandria, LA: Lamplighter Publications, 1958) 114.

11. *No Other Foundation* (Indianapolis, IN: Sure Foundation Publishers, 1965) 173-174.

Chapter Two

1. Vance Havner, *Messages on Revival* (Grand Rapids, MI: Baker Book House, 1989) 15-16.

2. Wood 39.

3. Olford 11-12.

4. Wood 39-40.

5. Selwyn Hughes, *Revival—Times of Refreshing* (CWR, 1990) 12.

6. Havner, *Hearts Afire* 103-104.

7. Hughes 13.

8. A. W. Tozer, *The Size Of The Soul* (Camp Hill, PA: Christian Publications, 1992) 12, 14-16.

9. Wood 43-44.

Chapter Three

1. Bob Mumford, *"The Father's Sentence of Death,"* Lifechangers: Raleigh, NC, 1992.

2. Oswald Chambers, *Disciples Indeed* (Fort Washington, PA: Christian Literature Crusade, 1960) 85.

3. Ken Gire, *Windows of the Soul* (Grand Rapids, MI: Zondervan Publishing House, 1996) 198.

Chapter Four

1. Edwin and Lillian Harvey, *They Knew Their God, Vol. 3* (Harvey and Tait, 1988) 95-96.

2. W. Hacking, *Smith Wigglesworth Remembered* (Tulsa, OK: Harrison House, Inc., 1981) 78.

3. Tozer, *The Pursuit of God* 12-13.

4. Tozer, *Leaning into the Wind* 29-30.

5. Samuel Chadwick, *The Way to Pentecost* (Fort Washington, PA: Christian Literature Crusade, 1976) 13.

6. Tozer, *Born After Midnight* 8-9.

Chapter Five

1. Vision Press, *The Harness of the Lord* (Marion, IA: tract) 2-5.

2. Norman Grubb, *Continuous Revival* (Fort Washington, PA: Christian Literature Crusade, 1985) 13.

3. Quoted by Robert Bellah, et. al., *Habits of the Heart* (Berkeley: University of California Press, 1985) 21.

4. Mickey Bonner, *Brokenness, the Forgotten Factor of Prayer* (Houston, TX: Mickey Bonner Evangelistic Association, 1995) 44.

Chapter Six

1. Alan E. Nelson, *Broken In The Right Place* (Nashville, TN: Thomas Nelson, Inc., 1994) 9-10.

2. Larry Crabb, *Men and Women* (Grand Rapids, MI: Zondervan, 1991) 80.

3. Wood 79.

4. Wood 79.

5. Nelson 62.

Chapter Seven

1. Jonathan Goforth, *By My Spirit* (Elkhart, IN: Bethel Publishing, 1983) 13, 20-23.

2. Grubb 23-24.

3. "The Lighter Side," *Basically Business Newsletter* (April, 1988) 1.

4. Tozer, Man—*The Dwelling Place of God* 102-103.

5. Michael L. Brown, *From Holy Laughter to Holy Fire* (Shippensburg, PA: Destiny Image Publishers, Inc., 1996) 90.

6. Olford 29-30.

7. Brown, *Whatever Happened to the Power of God?* 112.

8. Olford 71.

9. Brown, *Whatever Happened?* 116.

Chapter Eight

1. Brown, *Whatever Happened?* 160.

2 Leonard Ravenhill, *Revival God's Way* (Minneapolis, MN: Bethany House Publishers, 1983) 57.

3. Tozer, *The Best of A. W. Tozer* 101.

4. George Barna, *The Barna Report* 1994-1995: Virtual America (Ventura, CA: Regal Books, 1994) 85,83.

5. John Piper, *Future Grace* (Sisters, OR: Multnomah Books, 1995) 9.

6. Thomas A. Lambie, *A Bruised Reed* (New York: Loizeaux Brothers, 1953) 24-25.

Chapter Nine

1. P. J. Madden, *The Wigglesworth Standard* (Springdale, PA: Whitaker House, 1993) 17-18.

2. John G. Lake, *The John G. Lake Sermons on Dominion over Demons, Disease and Death*, ed. Gordon Lindsay (repr., Christ for the Nations, 1982) 68.

3. Smith Wigglesworth, *Ever Increasing Faith* (rev. ed., Gospel Publishing House, 1971) 99.

ANOTHER BOOK AVAILABLE FROM S.J. HILL

GOD'S COVENANT OF HEALING

"Is it God's will to heal His people?"

"Is healing really provided through the Atonement of Jesus Christ?"

"Should the last few verses of Mark 16 be included in the Bible?"

"Is there evidence of supernatural healing throughout Church history?"

"Are some people sick for the glory of God?"

"What about Paul's thorn in the flesh?"

"Why are some people not healed after receiving prayer?"

These and many other common questions are answered in **God's Covenant of Healing**.

This book contains a thorough study of the subject of divine healing in light of the Word of God.

S. J. HILL
P. O. BOX 918
GRANDVIEW, MO 64030